Rip's Book of...

Common Sense Selling

"Improving Sales Through Process Implementation"

Rip Walker

Published by Richard Walker, Charlotte, NC

ISBN: 1449595545

EAN13: 9781449595548

Library of Congress Control Number: 2009912745

Acknowledgements

"One of the greatest joys that I can receive, is the knowledge that I have helped others achieve their goals."

- Rip Walker

Every book has to have an acknowledgement page of some kind. A page dedicated to thank all of those for what I have become, and what I have achieved. Specifically, for the support that was needed to write, complete, and publish this book.

First, I thank my wonderful wife, Ladan. She has been at my side throughout the creation of this book and has always supported me when times were discouraging and frustrating. Her own inspirational story keeps me motivated to continue and develop when life kicks you in the teeth.

I wish to thank all the great people that have I met during my years at *Southeast Toyota Distributors, LLC.* It was a great ride, and I will always appreciate the opportunity that I was given to grow and develop as a person. Thank you Reggie Vaughn for seeing something in this car salesperson and hiring me in the first place.

I must recognize all the salespeople that I've learned from over the years. It was a very fortunate thing for me to be around and work with such a diverse, hard working group of salespeople in the southeastern region of the country. I will never forget these people. Thank you Uncle Frank, Joe, Orlando, Paul, Edi,

Sandra, Michelle, Leo, Bill, Rushie, Peter, Fernando, and so many more.

Thank you to my friends at *Toyota Motor Sales, U.S.A.* Doug Stevens and Greg Kitzens have been my friends there for over the past 20 years, and they have helped me many times during that period. Thank you!

And last, where would I be without my parents help, support, and love? Better parents cannot be found. The phrase, "I love you no matter what," holds sincere meaning for them. Whether I was right or wrong, they were always there to guide, encourage, and motivate me. I could never ask for better parents. I love both of you.

Thank you, thank you, and thank you all!

Rip Walker

Forward: Never Confuse Education With Intelligence

We all know people that have a great deal of education. We have friends, family, and clients that have their walls and offices adorned with degrees from various affluent schools and colleges.

But, does having a great deal of education mean that they are intelligent? Quite a few of those people actually are, so I don't want to say anything derogatory about them. However, I also know some doctors, politicians, and millionaires (Having money doesn't necessarily mean they're intelligent either.) who just aren't with the program.

A little while back I had an inflammation in my right arm. I went to my doctor to have him take a look at it. I was in an examination room and had just finished the usual pre-examination form completion rituals, when the doctor came in and asked me to take off my shirt. A young nurse walked in as well and stood next to me. I inhaled immediately to inflate my chest, hoping that I would look in better shape for the sake of the nurse and my pride.

The doctor then looked at my right arm from 15 feet across the room and said, "You have bursitis." Now bursitis is like a minor sports injury, a little ice and a little rest, and you'll be okay, but my arm was actually burning up with a skin temperature hot enough to melt wrought iron.

I exhaled as the nurse looked at me. We were both dumbfounded. This doctor was amazing! He could make a diagnosis from across the room. We asked him at the same time, "How do you know?"

He responded by asking us that if we saw our aunt walking down the street, how would we know it's our aunt? We didn't know where he was going with this. He continued, "You would just know." Mmmm… at this point I wondered if I should tell him about my uncle who is now my aunt? That's a different story.

In any case, he gave me some pain medication and sent me on my way. By the next day, my arm looked like a roasted leg of lamb, the redness had migrated around my arm, and it was heading upwards into my arm pit. What a contrast of colors there now was between my arm and the yellow *Jerry Garcia* tie that I was wearing that day.

It didn't look good and I needed a second opinion. I went back to the office and the doctor decided that he would prescribe some antibiotics, just in case there was an infection. He still didn't touch me, he just sat behind his desk.

As I was leaving, I ran into the other doctor in the practice. He took one look, grabbed my arm, and said that it was cellulites. In layman's terms, that means a staph infection.

If you know anything about staph infections you know that they can get pretty serious if left untreated. In other words, it could mean an extended vacation at the local hospital or indefinite stay in the local cemetery. By the way, I lived.

Where was the common sense with this doctor? He never was closer to me than 10 feet during my examination. He never laid a hand on me! All he had to do was feel my arm, and he would have recognized an infection. Then on second thought, maybe not. Needless to say he is no longer in the practice, and I hope he's given up medicine. He could have killed me.

Here's the point, a well educated doctor did not use his common sense. It's the same in life, many people don't use common sense, and if we don't use common sense when we sell, we could we kill sales.

With the ability to gather information of all kinds, most of our customers are well educated on our products.

In many cases, they don't just have model, feature, services, and other product information, they also have prices. It makes things competitive, but it also makes things very confusing. Education in the wrong hands can be dangerous!

I'm not saying that education is bad, I'm all for it. However, between misinformation and a lack of common sense it makes it tougher for us in sales. What are we to do?

What would be the common sense thing for us to do? We need to look at the whole sales process with common sense. Get educated ourselves, have a good understanding about the sales process, about ourselves, about people, and have some determination.

I'll use other stories to illustrate various points throughout this book. Some are true, some are made up, and some stories are embellishments of the truth. In other words, most of them are fictional, but many of the stories are similar to what we as salespeople run into every day.

I'm sure that everyone reading this book has a few stories of their own. Life is stranger than fiction. Back to our main thought.

Selling is not rocket science its common sense. This book will help you use yours to increase your sales!

Good Selling!

Rip Walker

- Tip 1. Never confuse education with intelligence.
- Tip 2. Get educated about the sales process.
- Tip 3. Have a good understanding about people.
- Tip 4. Use your common sense.

"Common sense ain't common."

- *Will Rodgers*

Table of Contents

<u>Section I: Common Sense Selling - Theory</u>

If you found this book on the shelf at your preferred retail bookstore, it was probably there among other books of the sales genre. Many are very similar, some are different. Some delve very specifically into one subject and some are pretty general.

I do some of that here as well. Quite frankly, some of the subjects deserve a big fat book of their own. I'll be writing some books about those further down the road.

Here, you are going to learn more about the process and the theory behind a sales process. You also will have a way to build your own sales process or at least understand and maybe improve the one that you have right now.

Theory without application won't produce anything except more thought. That's not a bad thing, but just trying to wing a sales process will get you dissatisfied customers along with a lot of heat and lost sales.

Theory is about what and why rather than the actual application. In this section, we deal with the theory behind a selling process. Why does something happen? What are we trying to achieve? The **"Why?"**

What and why are the themes that you will see repeated over and over and over. By knowing the what and why, you'll design a better process, you'll remember your process better, and you'll follow your process more consistently.

Having said that, a good sales process has many benefits. In the end, you'll serve your customers better, you'll sell more, you'll make more money, and you'll get less heat. Nothing like going to bed at night and not worrying about a lost sale or an upset customer. Wouldn't it be better to be thinking about a commission?

Let's get into this, let's start with the theory behind the sales process.

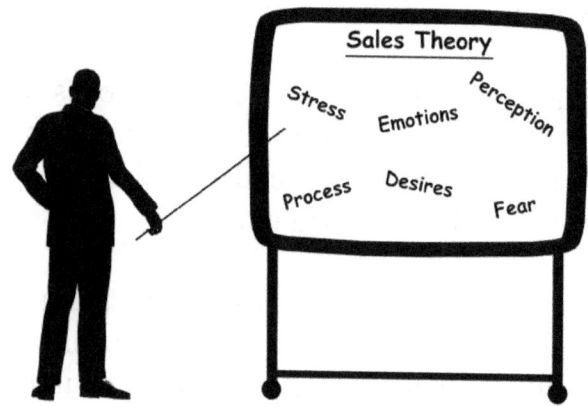

- Tip 5. Theory without application will only produce more thought.
- Tip 6. Theory is about what and why.
- Tip 7. Having a good process has many benefits.

*"Having a process is like having a map.
Without one you might get lost"*

- Rip Walker

Chapter 1: Have a Structured Sales Process

I used to travel, quite a bit, and I was always carrying electronic equipment of some kind with me. In my rush to get to the airport one early morning, I grabbed the wrong electric charger cord for my PDA.

When I arrived in California, the PDA needed charging so I hooked up the cord in my hotel room and went to an evening meeting. When I returned to my room, the PDA would not operate. I double checked everything and nothing worked. My PDA was dead.

A small diode light in the back of my head started blinking. Maybe I grabbed the wrong charger and fried this thing? The diode flashed brighter and more quickly. I then came up with this wonderful idea. I'll just call the PDA company and get it fixed under warranty. It shouldn't be a problem.

I went on the web, got the number to service, and made the call. I figured that it shouldn't take too long. Everybody does this right?

Jim, the customer service representative, picked up the phone. After he verified who I was and that I was the actual owner of the PDA, he delved deeper into the situation.

Here's how it went:

Jim: Mr. Walker, would it be okay to ask you a few more questions? We really want to make sure that we help you out as best as we can.

Rip: Sure go ahead, but I'm glad this thing is under warranty.

Jim: You said that the PDA was working yesterday?

Rip: Yep.

Jim: And it stopped operating after you charged it today?

Rip: Ah, yeah.

Jim: Then you would have the charger that you used with you?

Rip: (Suddenly feeling a little nervous.) Yeah, but what does that got to do with this?

Jim: Well, sometimes when people travel, they grab the wrong charger, and it could hurt the device. Would you mind getting it? I just would like to verify that it's the right charger.

Rip: (Getting really nervous.) Okay.

I already had the charger in my hand, and I was trying to figure out my next line of BS. I couldn't think of anything and this wasn't going in the right direction for me. I put the phone back to my ear and continued the conversation with Jim.

Rip: Okay, I have it.

Jim: Would you mind looking at the back of it for me and read the numbers off?

Rip: Okay…Just a minute…I'm sorry. (Thinking fast.) Oh, there's a bunch of numbers.

Jim: Just the one by where it says output. The ones in white.

Rip: Oh, those numbers. (Now cornered.) It says 7.5 V.

Jim: Oh, I'm sorry Mr. Walker. The right charger would say 5 V. It happens all the time sir. In a rush, you probably just grabbed the wrong charger didn't you?

Rip: (Now busted.) Yeah. I must have taken the wrong one.

Jim: We'll we still want you happy. We can fix it for $75. All we need is a valid credit card to get this started.

Rip: Okay.

You can't blame me for trying. What happened here? Jim had a process to follow. Do you think that this was the first time someone tried to get something fixed under a warranty when it was their fault a product broke, and it wasn't a defect in the product?

Do you suppose that Jim had some directions handy to tell him how to handle this issue? You better believe it! If there was a true product defect, I would have expected them to take care of the problem with no charge, but quite frankly, I fried the PDA on my own.

It's not that companies are never at fault, but some do minimize their losses, because they develop, train, and follow processes.

And just because they might have the financial means doesn't mean that people without common sense are allowed to reach into their coffers.

Just put yourself in their shoes. What if someone was walking across your lawn, fell down, and broke an ankle, would you want to pay for the doctor bills or for their lost wages? I don't think so.

In any case, great processes can prevent losses, but more important, they can increase sales, and improve the customer experience.

Whether its manufacturing, safety procedures, or selling, we need to have a well structured process to follow to be continually successful.

What is the structure of your process? Do you have one? Start thinking about your process for selling. What needs to happen? Where do you need to go with this process?

You are deciding what the directions will be for your process. It's your recipe, your manual, or your plan for selling. Good sales processes will have the same basics. They will all be structured.

By building a carefully thought out structured process, you can be more successful. Again, life will be easier for you, you'll make more sales, and your customers will be happier.

The gears of your mind should now be turning. Keep them turning and you'll find yourself with a great sales process.

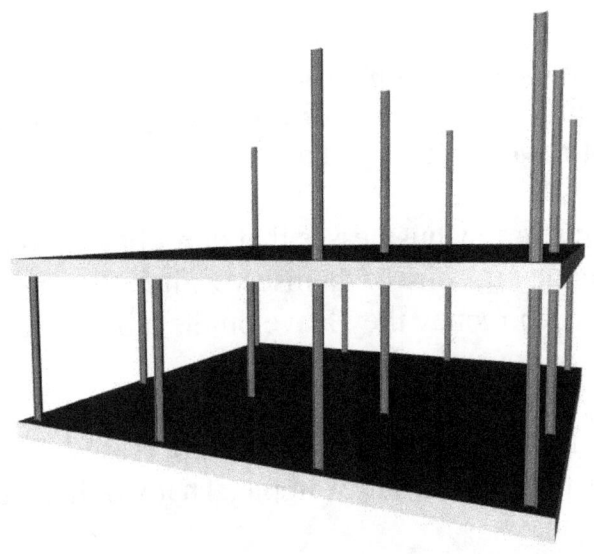

- Tip 8. It's common sense to have a structured sales process.
- Tip 9. Great processes lead to a great experience.
- Tip 10. Well structured processes lead to success.

"A building is but a pile of debris without structure."

- Rip Walker

Chapter 2: Understand the Basics of a Process

You may agree that it is important to have a process, and that you should follow one. However, what do you do if you are on your own or the outfit that you are with doesn't have one?

There are quite a few businesses that don't have good processes and make money in spite of themselves. It makes me wonder about how much money they leave on the table. You might have to design your own process.

Let's try to understand the basics of a process. We'll use a simple sales process for our example. That would be using common sense.

You can design your own "Road to the Sale" without much difficulty, although it might be tough to decide what you would like to include in it. You can use the example below as a format to build your own process later when we get into an application.

The ABC Car Dealership Sales Process

The Meet & Greet

1. The salesperson (SP) will wait inside until customers arrive. When a customer arrives, the SP will greet the customer wherever most convenient. That might be inside or outside.
   a. The idea is to help the customer relax.

2. SP greets the customer in the following manner:
   - Welcome to ABC Car Dealership.

- My name is (SP name) and I am a sales specialist.
- And your name is?
- Are you here for the "Ultra - Car Sale?" Use the name of whatever sale we are currently having.

a. This is done to be more professional.
b. A sale is mentioned, because it will strike an emotional note with the customer.
c. The SP will start trying to guide the customer through the process and affect their emotions by using a question which has been predetermined by the dealer and management. For example: Are you here for the "Ultra - Car Sale?"

Needs Assessment

1. SP will do this at their desk.
   a. We want our customers to relax.

2. The SP will ask several predetermined questions.
   - How will the car be driven?
   - What did you like about your last car?
   - What would you like in your new car?
   - What type of research have you done?
   a. By using effective predetermined open questions, information will be gathered more quickly.
   b. They are also more conversational.

Model Selection

1. The SP will recommend a vehicle to the customer based on the information from the needs assessment.
    a. Improper model selection is the largest reason for a "no sale." This is why it's so important to select the right vehicle in the beginning.

2. If the customer is in agreement, the SP will go get the vehicle and take the customer out.
    a. The SP is guiding the process.

3. If the customer does not agree, the SP will ask more questions to determine the right car. If the customer insists that they look at a car other than the one that is recommended, the SP will mention that they will be more than happy to, but it will most likely cost more money and the customer will need to be flexible.
    a. The SP is setting up a switch vehicle.

3. The SP takes the customer into the presentation part of the process.
    a. This continues the process.

Presentation

1. The presentation will be done on the lot.
    a. It keeps the customer on the car.

2. SP is to get keys.
    a. This allows the SP go to the sales desk and keep management aware of the customer's status.

3. SP is to have the customer logged prior to the demo drive.
    a. This is to help keep track of the customer and the deal.

4. SP pulls car out and does a presentation according to the ABC process.
    a. SP stays in control.

5. SP & Customer go on a demo drive.
    a. It is the next part of the process.
    b. This will help build value in the vehicle.
    c. A good demonstration will eliminate many objections.

Demonstration Drive

1. The SP will drive off the lot and make right turns.
    a. The customer is not familiar with the vehicle, and it is safer for the SP to drive first.

2. Management will be notified.
    a. This is for everyone's safety.
    b. It allows management to help track the process and where the SP is with the customer.

3. There can be exceptions to where the customer may drive off first, but again management must be notified.
    a. Again, for everybody's safety.

4. A copy of the customer's drivers license must be made prior to a demonstration drive.

a. This provides a degree of safety.
b. This is required by our insurance company.
c. It helps the dealership and the SP avoid liability.

5. SP is to follow the ABC demo drive process. See manual for complete steps.
   a. This maintains the flow of the process.

6. When the drive is completed the car is parked and the salesperson will do a trial close with the question," Is there anything that you need that is not in this vehicle?"
   a. It's time to see if the customer is on the right vehicle, and if they are sold on the car.

The Service Walk

1. Salesperson is to show the Service and Parts departments and present what the dealership has to offer. Let the customer know about the hours, the shuttle service and the free coffee.
   a. Sell yourself and the dealership! It's needed to build more value.

2. Use the "Put them on a Pedestal" format.
   a. It creates a great first impression with the Service and Parts departments.

Trade – In Valuation

1. SP is to do a silent walk around.
   a. We need this information to help close the deal later.

b. This helps a customer become more objective about their current vehicle.

2. SP writes up the appraisal form and brings it to the Used Car (UC) Manager, who appraises the vehicle.
   a. The UC Manager is responsible for the number on this vehicle.

3. SP and the customer sit at SP's desk and go over a "Why Buy Here Book."
   a. This keeps the customer busy, passes the time and helps build value in the dealership.

4. When the UC Manager returns, it is time for the write up and numbers.
   a. The write up is the next part of the process.

The Write Up, Negotiation, and Closing

1. The SP takes customer to an office or desk.
   a. It is more conducive.

2. The SP offers the customer a bathroom break and refreshments.
   a. The customer needs to relax to decide.

3. The SP gets any other information they need and then take their worksheet up to the desk.
   a. Sales managers are responsible for the numbers.

4. The SP presents the pricing menu to the customer and asks for the order.

a. You won't get the order if you don't ask.
b. You won't get the gross either.

5. The Customer says yes, continue onto delivery.
   a. It's the next step.

6. The customer says no. Be patient and ask why.
   a. To handle an objection you must know what it is. You must find out why the customer is not buying.
   b. Different objections need different answers.

7. SP continues to work on the deal and gets a manager to help if necessary.
   a. Use all means and good judgment to close the deal.
   b. Managers are there to sell cars also.

8. An agreement is reached with the customer on the price of the vehicle.
   a. This firms up the deal.
   b. Leads to step 10.

9. No agreement is reached and the customer is thanked and released by the SP.
   a. This helps set up customer follow up.
   b. By being non-confrontational, the customer will be more likely to return and buy.

10. The SP writes up a buyer's order.
    a. There isn't going to be a delivery if the customer does not agree on the vehicle and the financial terms.

11. A manager approves the deal.
     a. This helps reduce mistakes, which can cost money
        and hurt customer satisfaction.

Delivery

1. SP finishes the paperwork and gathers the buyer's order,
   the credit application, and a gas slip. SP gets the deal
   jacket and manuals.
     a. These documents are required for the purchase of a
        new vehicle and for proper vehicle registration.

2. SP goes to the desk and has the deal signed off on by a
   manager.
     a. To make sure that the numbers are right.

3. When the customer goes to the Finance Office, financing
   will be arranged.
     a. The customer needs to pay for the vehicle.

4. If the customer has to wait for F & I then the SP will go
   over the manuals.
     a. This occupies the customer and at the same time
        making the process seem shorter.

5. While the customer is in the Finance Office, the SP will
   complete input of customer information for follow up.
     a. This affects customer satisfaction.
     b. It affects future business for the dealer and the SP.

6. In either case, the SP needs to take the car to get ready.
     a. It's all part of the process.

b. The car needs to be made ready for the customer.

7. When the customer leaves the Finance Office, the manuals (If they have not been covered already.) and information in the delivery package are to be covered with the customer. Business cards are also placed into the package. The customer needs to become familiar with how their new vehicle will work.
    a. This improves customer satisfaction.
    b. This answers questions that the customer might have to ask dealership personnel later.
    c. Cards in the jacket help customers refer other people to the dealership and SP.

8. The customer is taken to their new vehicle, which is to be in the delivery area. It is located on the north side of the building, in the shade, away from other vehicles.
    a. A designated delivery area allows for a better final presentation of the vehicle to the customer.

9. If there is a trade in it will need to be checked in by the SP. The trade should also be parked close to the new vehicle.
    a. This makes it faster and easier to transfer license plates and customer belongings.
    b. Faster deliveries make everybody happier and more satisfied with the experience.

10. The SP will demonstrate the operation of the new vehicle to the customer. Any new issues are handled.
    a. A customer who is more knowledgeable about the operation of their vehicle is a more satisfied one.

b. If there are any issues, and they are handled now, the customer will be more satisfied.

11. At the end of the presentation the SP is to talk about the manufacturer's survey and explain that:
   a. The customer will receive a survey from the manufacturer over the next few weeks.
   b. It is a report card for the SP and the dealer.
   c. Their experience is very important to the dealership.
   d. Good is not excellent.
   e. If the customer is not 100% completely satisfied we need to know about it now.
   f. If there is anything that hasn't been excellent, the dealership will take care of it now.
   g. Are there any concerns?

12. The SP has the customer sign off on a delivery check sheet.
   a. This helps assure that things have been done right.

13. The SP thanks the customer for their business.
   a. This reassures the customer, relieves their tension and raises customer satisfaction.

14. The customer leaves in their new car.

Follow Up

1. The SP takes the trade to trade area and submits the keys and paperwork to the UC Manager.

a. Lost vehicles and misplaced paperwork create problems, frustration, and they cost time and money.

2. The SP sends a thank you e-mail/note to the customer the same day.
   a. This increases customer satisfaction and builds the relationship further.

3. The SP calls the next day and in 3 days and will continue contact on a schedule created by the PDC.
   a. This helps develop future sales.

This was an example format for writing a process. When you write out a process, you are writing out the directions.

It's a little different though than how some have described a process. I included the **"Why"** as in **"Why"** perform a specific part of the process.

Why did I include information other than the actual directions? People will perform better if they know the "**Why**."

This is what I'm trying to say:

"Professionals know what they do and why they do it that way."

When I was an automotive detailer, I used to have to install wheel caps, trim pieces, and mudguards. While I was installing a set of mud guards, I had to reach up under the wheel well to loosen a few screws. I felt something scratch the back of my hand. I pulled it out and had to administer some first aid. Somehow I had cut the back of my hand wide open.

I took a look under the wheel well and there was an exposed, jagged piece of sheet metal where I had cut my hand. It seemed out of place, so I checked the same spot on a few other of the same model vehicles. No other sheet metal was exposed like this. Nothing there to cut anybody.

I could have let it die there, but being the curious guy I was, I made a few calls to the factory. Lo and behold, there was a new guy installing wheel well liners the wrong way. He didn't follow the directions. He didn't follow them because he didn't know why the liners were to be installed in an unexposed position.

If he had known that people were going to chew up their hands in the wheel wells because of what he did, he may have installed the part in the proper position. I didn't cut my hands on any more of these, so he probably got the message.

Again, **"Professionals know what they do and why they do it that way!"**

When you design a process always remember to include the **"Why."** It's common sense.

I just want to make a side note, if you are going to build a sales process or any process, for that matter, with more than just you doing the selling, you had better get people on the front line involved for several reasons.

The main one is for a new process to work, you will need to have the buy-in from the participants. A secondary reason is that they might know how to do something better than you.

Many companies have tried to put a great process in place, but have failed, all because the people who were to follow it were never involved in its creation. Again, just a thought and with it, common sense.

For more insight into this please, get a copy of *The Toyota Way*. It goes into the great efforts that Toyota does to make its manufacturing process the best in the business and don't take my word for it, just look at their cars' reputation for quality.

How do you decide what to include in your process? It depends, but mostly you have to ask, what do I want to achieve with this process? What is my or my group's goal?

Our final goal is to make the sale, but what else? Keep in mind that every part of a sales process has a goal. If there isn't a reason for the step or action, it doesn't need to be included it's just extraneous.

Just as I included the **"Why"** in my example, you need to think about what and why to put a good process together. Break the entire process down into smaller steps or smaller processes and it will be easier.

As an example let's look at objection handling. Assume that you have followed a great sales process to a T, and that you haven't had any objections until you have presented numbers and have asked for the sale.

The customer says no or says they need to check with someone else, or they're not ready or whatever. What is the first thing you want to do? We know that we want to overcome the objection. What do we say and what do we do?

We need to think through this and know what's going on. We have to find out why they are not buying at this moment. Maybe they do need someone else to make the decision, but we should have found that out a long time ago. **"Why?"** There's that question again. We need to really know why they aren't proceeding to buy.

We know that we have to ask why as part of this process, but an experienced professional will also know that at this point the customer's stress level is probably at its peak. We need to soften this process to get the information that we need.

People under stress usually don't make decisions, unless they have to or are forced to. If someone buys under either situation, the deal will either fall down later, or they will be unsatisfied customers. So another part of this process would be to get the customer to relax.

First, why are they so uptight? It's mostly just fear of the unknown. Is it the right purchase? Am I paying too much? Do I really like this? Will it do the job? They don't have enough information or they don't have the right information. It's our job to get it for them.

It's like when we stall going to a doctor for a checkup. I had this mole on my head for over two years. I knew that I should go to a dermatologist for a look. (Yes, I'm bald.) I finally did

21

and you know what? It was nothing! However, we know in some cases it could have been.

I allowed fear to stop me from making a decision. Okay, now back to the customer and stress. They need more information to calm their fears, but we don't know what to give them. We have to find out what to give them.

First, let's let the customer know that we heard them by acknowledging what they said. And to change their state of mind a bit.

Salesperson: I understand that you said no?

Customer: Yes.

Salesperson: That's okay. You don't have to buy anything right now. But, if you wouldn't mind I'd like to ask you a question? (Sounds like the Jim, the PDA guy.)

Customer: Okay.

Salesperson: Is there something more specific that you can tell me? Is there something about the car that didn't fit right? Are there questions that I haven't answered?

Customer: I didn't like the color.

Salesperson: What color would you like?

Customer: A dark gray one.

Salesperson: What you are saying is that if the car was dark gray you would order it?

Customer: Well, yeah.

Salesperson: No problem Mr. Customer. I'll get you one. Just sign here and press hard, its five copies...

I'm not going any further at this point, and I wanted to keep it real simple. The point is, in this process we wanted to dig deeper while at the same time keeping it conversational and letting the customer relax by easing their fears.

It's also wise to ask questions that your customer can answer yes to. It's a psychological thing. The customer has gotten it in their mind to say no, but you have to allow them to reprogram themselves to say yes. With the right questions, they can answer yes to you, which is a good thing when selling.

For now, understanding the basics of a process is common sense. Take a look at the objection handling example here and the PDA service experience from earlier. They are similar in process, but different in content.

Both are structured processes and both use some type of fact finding in their process to handle the objection and get the sale. How about that? What you will find is that the basics of a sales process are the same. I know that I'm repeating it, but it's so the point will sink in.

Let's go further and take a look at the buying process, which is different from a selling process.

- Tip 11. People can't make decisions if they aren't relaxed.
- Tip 12. People need to know the **"Why"** part of a process.
- Tip 13. Design questions for a yes.

"Before anything else, preparation is the key to success."

-   Alexander Graham Bell

Chapter 3: Understand the Buying Process

No, I didn't mean to say selling process. Again, the buying process is different than a selling process. It's about why people buy, not how you sell. Although, you do need to understand buying and how you might be able to tailor your sales process towards buying to make it more effective.

It's common sense to understand the buying process. If you really know where a customer is coming from you can build a relationship better and sell better.

The buying process can be long or short. It might be an impulse purchase at the counter of a quick mart, I want a candy bar, or it might be longer, I think we need a new car. Even though both purchases take different amounts of time, they basically have the same process. A need or a want is developed or created.

People have a need and someone tries to fill it. Back at the Quick Mart, I see a candy bar at the counter; my mouth may start to water. A want or need is created. It's not much money. I decide to fill the need by paying the dollar and inhaling the candy bar in two bites. Yes, I did take the wrapper off. I like the new chocolate *Hershey* bar with no foil to slow down my eating. My need is filled.

How about a car? Some people say that people buy a car in three days. In some cases, that's true. Your 16 year old daughter decides to go four wheeling with your mini-van on the golf course one night with her friends, and it turns into a boat charter in the pond by the 4th hole. No one dies or gets injured, but because cars don't do to well under water, you need a new car ASAP.

The process starts. Other than submarining a car, there can be other things that create a need or want.

Physical Needs

Maslow had a hierarchy of needs. I believe that some of the ones on the bottom of the pyramid include food, water, and sex. We get hungry we eat. We get thirsty we drink. We get....... We try to satisfy our needs and wants.

But, what about the buying process for products and services? What about the things that might fulfill other needs? Things that are a little higher on the pyramid.

The things that I am referring to are not necessarily for survival. For example; My teenage daughter watches a kid's reality show and sees clothes from the latest fashion trend, and I hear, "Daddy all the girls at school have them, and I'll just die if I don't get them! Daddy! Pleeeasee?"

Or, why buy dinner for your family at a *Ruth's Chris Steak House*, when for 15% of the cost you can buy steaks at the store and grill them at home. By the way, they do make a great steak!

Yes, food is needed for survival, but I don't think that I'll die if I eat at home. Unless of course I let my neighbors bring over rare chicken for us to eat again. Raw is for sushi not for chicken.

Other physical needs to survive might be a wheel chair, oxygen tanks, medical supplies, and you get the idea. Services also can be physical needs. A package needs to be delivered, a product needs to be manufactured, and on we go.

Emotional Needs

This is the part of the book where we talk about our feelings, so don't get mushy. We all like to feel good. This is an emotional need that we all have. We can fill this need in different ways, but let's stay within legal boundaries.

For example, the candy bar at the quick mart stopped my mouth from watering and gave me a chocolate high. The loaded *Toyota Sequoia* helped my ex-wife feel better about her image around the neighbors, while at the same time it created a need for me to think about taking a second job at a local restaurant to help pay for it. Fear of losing my house need.

Emotional needs fall into a few categories:

Self Image
Peace of Mind
It Gets Me Excited

Self Image

Self image is about how we think we look to ourselves and to others. In most cases the views are totally different, but what is important is our perception of what we think other people think about us. Did you get that?

A few years back, my family and I lived in Boca Raton, Florida, an affluent area where the median income is well above most of the country. We lived in the lesser affluent area next to the everglades. We used a lot of insect repellant and avoided swimming in the community ponds for fear of alligators and snakes.

Returning to self image. Quite a few people around Boca Raton have luxury vehicles. The ones that were the most popular, when I lived there and before it became trendy to have a hybrid, were LSAVs, large suburban assault vehicles. The *Cadillac Escalade*, the *Hummer*, the *Toyota Land Cruiser* were all standard fare in Boca. They are all sweet rides and 4 wheel drive.

But, why 4 wheel drive? Ask and people will say something like, "I drive up north, or I go skiing in the winter in Colorado." Yeah right. If they have the money to afford these vehicles most likely they will be taking a plane first class to get to their destination and not driving.

The only other reason is for the impending ice age which is due in about another 100,000 years. Don't believe everything that you hear about global warming. That's most likely a part of another emotional sales pitch to get more tax dollars from you and me. Most politicians use fear to get votes and that includes all political parties. Negative selling, but selling it is.

Okay, so why? It goes back to how we will feel when others look at us.

A few years ago, I was training salespeople in Greenville, South Carolina about the fine attributes of a *Toyota Land Cruiser*. A *Land Cruiser* is the top of the line *Toyota*. It's large and loaded with a price tag of about 60k to 70k dollars. I could not afford to buy this car or the gas for it, unless thousands buy this book, and I get some speaking engagements.

After the training, I needed to drive from Greenville to Columbia, South Carolina, the state capitol. I took interstate 26, which would mean about a two hour drive.

As I drove down the highway, I noticed that this burgundy *Land Cruiser* was an awesome ride. It had all the amenities including leather, a great stereo system, and a power sunroof.

After I drove for a while, I noticed a late model, paneled station wagon coming up to pass me. I haven't seen one of those in 25 years. It started to pull up beside me, and I saw a young boy staring up at me. It was my perception, but it was really the *Land Cruiser* he was looking at.

Then the boy tapped his mother in the passenger front seat, and he pointed over to me. Again my perception. Everyone in the wagon was looking...up at me...while I was looking... dooowwwnnn at them.

All I could say in my mind was, "Yes, it's my *Land Cruiser*! Yes, you think I have money! Look at me! I am so great!"

Underneath, I was saying, "They think it's me, but it's all B.!!!#@@### % S.$$#@#@! But, boy this feels pretty good!"

This is called snob appeal. I don't classify myself as someone above everybody. Everybody's blood is red when they get cut. In this world, we are all in it together and no one gets out alive! You might remember this when you start getting snobby.

No one should feel that they are a better person than their neighbor, just because they have more money. However, I would have no problem using self image to help me sell something, and you shouldn't either.

There's no problem pitching to self image at all. If you doubt me, just watch some of the television advertisements. What do cosmetic ads say? What about many of the car ads? What about clothing ads?

There is nothing wrong with making someone feel better about themselves as long as it's legal and ethical. You don't even need to make money on the deal.

Compliment your wife, kids, friends, or co-workers sincerely and specifically on something that they did and watch the smile that they give you. It's priceless and it will make you feel pretty warm and fuzzy as well.

As far as using this in sales, you have to find out how important self image is to the customer. I sold a late model, lime green *Honda Civic* to a repeat customer over the phone. The car had over 150,000 miles on it, but it ran well. It was cheap and it was ugly. Honestly, I looked up the word ugly in the dictionary and next to it was a picture of this car. Okay, old joke.

I told the customer about the car's appearance. He didn't care, he just wanted some cheap transportation for driving around NYC.

His image didn't matter. He bought the car sight unseen and drove off happily with his purchase. His biggest need was to get something reliable that nobody would want to steal. He wanted some peace of mind. By the way, it did get stolen later.

Peace of Mind

People will pay big money for this. The proof is life insurance. Let's get this straight, I pay premiums for years in the hopes that I don't ever get to collect? With life insurance, you are actually going to need to die to collect. If you die you will not be caring about anything anymore.

We all know the deal. We want some peace of mind right now. If we depart from this world prematurely, (And when would it not be premature?) we don't want our loved ones to suffer financially after we are gone.

Life insurance is not a bad thing. I have some coverage, because I do care about my family. My fear is that as the plane I'm in is going down, I don't want the last thing going through my head, aside from a piece of the landing gear, is that my family is going to suffer because of my death.

There are similar things like this that people will pay additional to have peace of mind. I bought a car for my then teenage son a few years ago. It was one of the first ones with side curtain airbags.

That feature was about $800 additional, but my fear was that someone would T-bone him and all that would be between the thinnest part of his young skull and the raised bumper of an over accessorized 4 wheel drive (Remember the LSAVs.) would be about a quarter inch of tempered safety glass. Did I paint a picture for you?

I didn't want to receive the tragic call in the middle of the night and not have done everything that I could have done to protect him. I paid the money with a smile on my face. People will pay for peace of mind. What have you purchased for peace of mind?

It Gets Me Excited

Why would someone pay millions to ride on top of a *Soyuz* rocket? My bet is one to four hundred that there will be a catastrophic failure of some kind, and you will return as a wish for someone. Please, see the previous section on life insurance.

Would you put a gun to your head with those odds? Would you pay to do that? Maybe not, but yet there are people who pay for the thrill. That's why experience type vacations are so big now. That's also why we have roller coasters. We love to get excited, and I mean that in a good way.

With customers, you have to find out how to thrill them. This doesn't mean to do something dangerous. We'll dig deeper into thrilling them in the chapter on tying into emotions.

PSYCHOLOGY 101.

- Tip 14. People make decisions based on their emotions.
- Tip 15. People can have physical and emotional needs.
- Tip 16. We need to understand our customer's emotions.
- Tip 17. People will pay for peace of mind.
- Tip 18. People want to be thrilled.

"The noblest pleasure is the joy of understanding."

- Leonardo Da Vinci

Chapter 4: Tie Into the Emotions of Your Customer

There was an insurance salesperson I knew a few years ago. He was a sharp guy, professional, and a soft seller. Now if you ever sold insurance or know about it, it can be a tough business. However, this guy knew how to tap into a customer's emotions, and he became very successful.

He would first try to put his customers at ease. He would chat a little, build some rapport, and then get into the presentation. He would use the brochures, diagrams, and statistics to set up the close. Keep in mind that he would do his job and recommend a product that fits his customers' needs.

He knew the process, he knew where in the process that people would object, and he knew how to answer all the various objections. And then he would use a story to close the deal. The story might go like the one below.

His customers, Bill and Jill, would be sitting together on the couch. My friend would be across from them. His customers would have balked and stalled. My friend would have answered all of their questions.

He then told the story, and it would go like this… Bill, I know that you're concerned about your family and what would happen to them if you were gone. Jill and Bill would nod in agreement.

Many people like yourselves are considering life insurance and most are selecting a program that fits their needs. They nod again.

However, I would like to share something with you that happened to me a few years ago, when I was just starting in the business. They nod again and he goes into his story.

I was with a fine young couple just like you. And they wanted to think about it. I said okay, no problem. I called them a few days later, and they wanted me to come back over Monday afternoon, after the weekend, to choose and sign up for a program.

When I went over the next Monday, I found that it was a little tough to park. It seemed that the street was crowded with cars. I walked up the steps and rung the door bell.

The woman of the house answered the door. She had been crying. She apologized for not calling me, and then she told me how her husband was killed on the highway Saturday night. I expressed my condolences and then she asked me for a favor.

For dramatic effect, my friend paused for a second. Bill and Jill have now moved very close together, and they are both on the end of their seats. Jill's hand is gouging into Bill's thigh, and he can't feel a thing.

My friend continued. She asked me if I could post date a contract and have her "Husband" sign. I don't blame her for asking, and I had to tell her no, but I don't ever want that to happen again. Jill's eyes are watering and Bill's mouth is hanging open.

My friend hands a pen to Bill. You said that you want to protect your family. Bill looks at Jill. Jill then nods at Bill. Deal closed.

My friend used a story to open up and tie into his customer's emotions. Let's take a look at a few other ways to touch a person on an emotional level.

First, how do people take information in? They take information in through their five senses. Touch, taste, sight, sound and smell. I consider smell and taste almost the same, so I'll discuss them together.

Any connection through these senses can be very, very powerful. If the connection is used correctly, results can be absolutely amazing. That's not just for sales, but in our other relationships as well.

I'm going to give you a story and then analysis the use of senses in the presentation with the customer.

The *BMW* Test Drive

I drove off of the lot with Mr. Jones in a *BMW* all-wheel-drive sport sedan. We drove about a half mile down the road and took a hard right turn onto a wooded, but paved back road. I could feel my weight shift as I turned and could hear the engine rev as I shifted gears. Mr. Jones grabbed the passenger handhold tightly.

I kept the car in a lower gear, so we could accelerate faster up the hill. Our backs were pushed into the rear of the seats. I hit a straight away and punched it. We never broke the speed limit of 55 miles per hour, but the narrow road and the nearby trees gave us the perception that we were going much faster.

We finally made another hard turn and found my predetermined spot to exchange seats. I told him that I was going to slam on the brakes, so he could see how the ABS system worked. Mr. Jones held onto the passenger assist handle tightly with white faced knuckles as we stopped.

We got out of the car and did an admiration walk around the "Beemer." It was a pretty sight. A well defined sports car with a large field and beautiful pine trees around us. It was a picture right out of the brochures, and we could just hear the muscular sound of the engine idling. We stood in front of the *BMW* to admire it for a few moments.

Mr. Jones then hopped into the driver's seat. He buckled his seat belt, and I then helped him adjust his seat and tighten his seat belt another two inches. He nervously laughed as I told him that I didn't want him to slide out on some of the turns we would be taking. I also told him that he would quit before the car did. As we drove off, I started the CD for a little music to set the mood.

As he pulled out and hit a straight away, I made him push the pedal down. A smile spread across his face. I then had him take some turns and not apply the brake. Of course I knew just how fast we could go. From there he got more comfortable. We zipped in and out of the corners and between the trees.

Finally, we came back to the dealership and parked by his trade at the front of the showroom. Funny, when he got out of the car, he could see himself in car in the reflection of the showroom glass. This gave him a visual comparison of the new car and his old one. He exhaled. Who wants an old car anyway?

Okay, enough story. Everything that I did here had a reason and all the senses were touched. On an individual basis, here's what happened.

Touch

It might be obvious, but by taking hard turns, accelerating quickly, and stopping hard I had the customer feel things through touch. His weight shifted in different ways that he wasn't used to. Probably, the only time he's felt his body do these things was on a roller coaster or in a malfunctioning elevator.

That would be called sense memory. That's when you experience something different that has similar physical traits of something in the past and the emotions from that experience come back to you.

Did Mr. Jones like the roller coaster when he was twelve? I'll bet he liked the *BMW* coaster ride I gave him as well at 40. Do you think that tightening his seat belt did anything? They use seat belts on roller coasters don't they? You get the idea.

Of course Mr. Jones also got to touch the leather steering wheel and feel the breeze as we did our test drive. I'll bet he felt that he was in a *BMW* commercial.

For another example of using touch, just go into an *APPLE Store* in the mall. The people are getting an emotional kick from playing on all the gadgets. Yes, sight and sound also play a part in it as well. It works well for *APPLE,* because when I pass by their stores in the mall, they're always crowded.

Get your customer to feel what you are offering them. That's why it's so important to get their hands on whatever it is you are selling. Have them try on the clothes, put the headset on, play the video game, lift the pot or sit on the couch.

Start thinking about how you will get to their emotions by getting them physically involved with your product or service.

Taste and Smell

Mr. Jones certainly got a nose full of new car smell. Funny how a combination of plastic, metal, fiberglass, various chemicals, and fumes can make us feel so good, but so be it. People love the smell of new cars and products.

Aside from the new car smell, what else did he inhale other than the car's exhaust? The pine trees, the field, the flowers, and etc. He also smelled my mint gum that I was chewing.

I want the customer to smell something positive and not the pepperoni pizza that I had for lunch. That's an important thought.

This is all psychological. I want the customer to feel good and to relax. By putting them in a positive state of mind, I stand a better chance of closing the deal.

What about in your case? Is there an apple pie, that's been cooked, sitting on the kitchen table at the open house? Can people smell the steak cooking in the restaurant? Does your store smell clean and professional? What about your own hygiene?

I think you get the point. Get to their emotions in a positive way by use of taste and smell.

Sight

What did our customer see on this drive? He saw the fine lines of a luxury automobile in a beautiful brochure type setting. That's a lot better than having the car nestled in with another 100 somewhat similar cars isn't it? It kind of makes what I'm selling stand out better.

The trees flashed by on the drive. It gave the impression to the customer of traveling much faster. Just an illusion, but the senses didn't know it.

And *BMW* did a great job on the design of the interior as well. I think that all that research and development paid off. Yeah, I do like their style.

What do your customers see in your selling world? All positive? Things are organized and merchandised properly? Are all the cameras and computers working in your electronic store? Are the big screens on with football games or action movies playing in HD? Think about how your client will see your product in the best light. Does your customer have a way that they can see themselves enjoying your product or service?

Sound

Mr. Jones heard all kinds of things didn't he? The exhaust running. The growling rumble of the engine and the wind going by. All of these affected his perception of speed and got to his emotions. They got his heart racing and put a big smile on his face.

The other thing that I did was to put on some music. Music is very powerful. It can touch our soul and can affect our emotions tremendously. As a warning, be very careful of what music you play for your customers. Not everybody is into *Neil Diamond*.

Most stores have strategically chosen music to fit most of their targeted markets and make the selling environment more conducive. Take *Abercrombie and Fitch*, for example; I walk into the store and can't hear a thing.

However, their young to early twenty year old market loves to hear ear drum busting base with lyrics that no one can understand. They should put in a couple of lounge chairs in a sound deadening area for guys like me. They seem to forget that my generation is the one that usually pays for their stuff.

All kidding aside, they are a successful operation, and they know how to use most of our senses to get to our emotions. Especially through sound.

How does your sales environment sound? Are audio displays working? Is there sale conducive music over the PA? Is the sales staff using sound to help sell?

What's left?

Maybe you've heard the term, "Paint them a picture." This should probably fall under the sight sense because we are actually having customers see a picture in their mind. It's very important and deserves a section of its own.

"Painting a picture," refers to telling stories, like the ones I've shared with you. You tell the customer a story that makes your selling point and allows the customer to relate to the subject in the story and maybe put themselves in it.

This is what I did with the *BMW* test drive story. I wanted my readers to see what I was doing and make my point. I can't take everyone out on a test drive with me, but I can take you mentally with a good story.

If what you are selling is not something that you can show physically, you're going to need to paint a picture of your own. Tell a story about how the service that you are selling saved a client a huge amount of money or how they enjoy life better now that they have the service. Paint a picture with them enjoying the benefits. It's just a story.

Stories can be long, like the ones that I have used or very short. An example of a short story might be, "Would you like to see that car in your driveway?" Or, when a real estate salesperson says, "Can you see you and your family enjoying a bar-b-q in this backyard?" Or when a banker says, "Just imagine what you'll do on your retirement with the annuity funds."

If you use questions with your story, you also get the customer to interact with you and interaction helps create a better experience.

It's all pretty simple, but it does take some preparation and thought to use a story to tie into emotions through the senses. You just need to work at developing your skills in regard to this.

Professionals with common sense know how to use the senses to tie into emotions. Be aware of a customer's senses and utilize them.

- Tip 19. Tie into your customer's emotions.
- Tip 20. Use the five senses to touch emotions.
- Tip 21. Use stories and paint pictures.
- Tip 22. Have an effective presentation.
- Tip 23. Get your customer involved.
- Tip 24. Prepare your presentation.

"No law or ordinance is mightier than understanding."

- Plato

Chapter 5: Solve Problems for Your Customer

Salespeople solve customer problems. That's what we really do. We find a need, a want, or something that needs to be solved, and we try to "fix" it. The better the job you are at solving problems the better the salesperson that you will be.

I used to go to a dentist in West Boca Raton. She was polite and professional, but not a problem solver. I was having a checkup done, and she came back into the room with some x-rays. She looked at them and looked at me.

Now keep in mind that I was in a very vulnerable position. I was on the chair with my mouth wired wide open, with all the neat accessories that a dentist sticks into your mouth, and then charges you for the experience.

She started to tell me that I needed a root canal, a new crown, and whatever else. My thoughts went to the fact that it was near the end of the year where my benefits would run out, and I would have to pull money out of my pocket. Christmas was coming up and I started to get worried.

She must have been thinking about Christmas too. She got so excited when she told me what I would need. It was like listening to a six year old run down their Christmas list for Santa Claus. It almost brought a tear to my eye. Maybe the *Novocain* was wearing off?

I asked her what this would run. She told me in the neighborhood of two thousand dollars and that really made me cry. Maybe I would pull the tooth myself?

What about my Christmas budget? I asked her what she could do about the bill. With my mouth being held open by some stainless steel pliers of some kind, I guess she couldn't understand me very well.

The next few moments were a blur. I was escorted to the office administrator up front, who would make an appointment for the root canal, the crown, and the follow up visit. I think that this is called the bum's rush. This dentist didn't even look me in the eye. This is a bad thing when they won't look you in the eye.

It took me a couple of hours to sort this out. I later called and canceled the appointments. I then got a referral from someone at my office for another dentist, so I could get a second opinion.

The examination at my new dentist came up with the same diagnosis, but this dentist was a problem solver. He broke up the procedures over December of the current year and January of the coming year. I didn't have to front a dime. He got the sale because he was a problem solver. Merry Christmas! He used some common sense.

Become a great problem solver and your customers will love you. How do you become a problem solver? Let's run through a few things to help you get some ideas for your process for solving problems in your line of work.

The basics, first you have to identify the problem or need. We do that by fact finding. Some people call it a needs assessment, discovery, customer consultation, or something else with a long title. In any case, you may need to do some research. Maybe hit the books, the web, or a company web site to get the information that you need. It really depends on your business. In any business, you'll need to develop good questions and really find and identify the need, want, or problem.

What Are Good Questions?

Good questions are questions that are designed to get the most accurate and best information possible without working too hard. They have to be efficient and appropriate for what you are trying to find.

Don't ask a customer what their dress size is if they're shopping for a refrigerator. They might be the same size, but it would still be irrelevant. I know that's an extreme example, but remember that this book is about common sense.

There are also basic types of questions. Open and closed. Neither type is good nor bad and they both have their place in this process. It's best to figure out what questions to ask and where to ask them before trying them out on a customer.

Closed Questions

Closed questions are ones, which are usually very direct and the response that they bring is usually very short.

- Do you like the color? Features? Feel? Look? Fit?
- Are you ready to buy?
- Do you want a large washer?
- Who's the car for?
- Does it hurt here?
- Do you like how it sounds?

- Are there any other TVs you liked?

You get the idea. Again, nothing bad with a closed question and there are times to use one, but let's use common sense and get efficient.

Open Questions

With a good technique, open questions will draw out more information in a shorter time, making the sales process easier and better flowing.

Remember that you want to lower your customer's stress level. A good grilling of twenty questions will get them taking extra *Diovan*. That's a blood pressure medication for those of you in the under 30 crowd. Don't interrogate your customer by firing off a bunch of questions! You want to make it conversational.

You'll need to design some open questions that fit into your sales process. Here are some examples of open questions:

- What type of vehicle are you looking for?
- What doesn't your current washer do that you would like your new washer to do?
- How will the copier be used?
- Tell me about the pain?
- Tell me what you think of the sound?
- What features have you seen on TVs, stereos, computers,… that you liked?

Odd, some of these questions sound a lot like the closed questions I mentioned before. I guess with a few different words we can make them open. How about that?

Think about the questions that you currently ask. Are they closed or open? Can you make them open? Can you design them to be more effective? Remember to be conversational when asking questions.

In the discovery chapter, you'll get a chance to design effective questions and a process for asking them, but for now we should probably talk about communication. That's the next chapter, but here are a few tips first.

$$2 + 2 = 4$$

- Tip 25. Good questions are efficient and appropriate.
- Tip 26. Be conversational when asking questions.
- Tip 27. Don't interrogate your customer.
- Tip 28. Look to become a problem solver.

"Problems bring opportunities."

- *Rip Walker*

Chapter 6: Communicate Effectively With Your Customer

Some people are gifted in this area. Wasn't *Ronald Reagan* the "Great Communicator?" Just about everybody liked him, and he had many good attributes. He was very talented.

Unfortunately, most of us aren't as good. Half the people who get married, get divorced. I don't know many are recycled over and over, but from what I read and hear, it's lack of communication or bad communication. I'm married for the second time, so I'm allowed to say these things.

Many people don't understand each other, especially when they first get married. I had the same problem with my first marriage, but that story would be long and very scary. I'll save it for the movie.

I once knew someone who dated a girl for over a year. They fell in love and decided to get married. I understand it was a great party. The couple went on a honeymoon in the Bahamas and returned after a week to their new home in Savannah, Georgia. Everything was just wonderful.

It wasn't until the very first Sunday, that they were husband and wife, that they started to communicate effectively. It just happened to be the opening day for the *Atlanta Falcons* football team.

Tom, not his real name, had just settled down in his *Lay-Z-Boy* in front of his new *Sony* HD 60" flat screen TV. There were chips and salsa on the table and a cold and frosty beer in the chair cup holder.

The first sip of beer hit his taste buds. He followed it with a mouthful of chips and was sinking into the recliner further when his young wife quietly snuck up on him from behind. Just like a mountain lion stalking its prey.

The conversation went something like this: "Honey, I love you," She said.

"I love you too," He responded, without turning his head.

His southern bell wife from Macon, Georgia kneeled down next to him.

She asked him, "Are you enjoying the game honey?"

Not looking, Tom said, "Yes, I am."

She continued, "That's great!"

His ears started to perk up. Her next words would stun him and cause him to inhale a tortilla chip.

She said, "Because, you won't be able to watch football on Sunday anymore after today."

Now she had his attention. He slowly turned his head toward her as she spoke. He had salsa dripping from his chin, which fell onto his official *Atlanta Falcon* football shirt. The stain would forever serve as a reminder of what happened that day.

On she went, "We're going to be spending our entire day at church on Sunday."

Tom thought, "Is this for real?"

She planted the knife deeper into him, "And you won't be able to work late at your job either, because we'll be spending most of our evenings at the church as well."

Tom's mind was overwhelmed as she went on and twisted the jagged blade deep into his heart, "And those friends of yours, you won't be seeing much of them from this moment forward either."

At this point, the details on the police report became unclear as to what happened next, but Monday morning she was on her way back to her parents in Macon via the local bus line.

What happened? All of this could have been avoided by just a little better communication, prior to the ring ceremony.

I think that everybody knows this, but communicating effectively for most of us is hard work. Let's talk about some ways to communicate effectively.

Most communication between people is by non-verbal and verbal means. (Telepathy will be in another book.) We'll discuss both, but since most of what we learn or pick up is from non-verbals, we'll discuss them first.

<u>Non-Verbal Communication</u>

Non-Verbals relate, for the most part, to our appearance and body language. The key areas for non-verbals are; our dress, our posture, our gestures and most important our facial expressions including eye contact.

What I will do here is break them down individually and give you some examples of how to use them effectively.

How We Dress and Overall Appearance

One of the first things that your customer is going to see is your overall appearance and how you dress. The way that you dress will depend on your type of sales position.

If you sell high end products, jewelry, homes, cars or business to business solutions, you're probably going to be in a suit or some other business attire. If you work at *Best Buy* or *Chili's* a clean sport shirt, which these chains usually supply, is the most likely option. If you are selling pest control you'll want to have a clean uniform and those little paper shoe covers when you walk into a customer's house. Use your common sense.

A professional appearance is necessary in all cases, but you can also alter your appearance to help you stand out and sell better.

For example, in one dealership that I used to call on, there was one salesperson who always wore a suit and tie. It wasn't required and the other salespeople all dressed nicely, but I could stand back and watch and see people walk in and go directly to him.

Many thought he was a manager, or maybe he just looked more professional. No wonder he was one of the top car salespeople in the country.

Unfortunately, people don't usually follow the rule about don't judge a book by its cover. You might find it hard to believe, but even as charming and as handsome as I am, some people don't' feel comfortable with middle aged bald guys. I think that hair is overrated anyway.

The point is, look at your appearance and be professional. Remember that not everybody will warm up to you and don't take it personal.

Think about how you dress? What does it say about you? Think about how to dress and how you can help your sales by wearing the right type of clothes.

Posture and Gestures

I arrived at a dealership early one day and set up my things in the meeting room. I got a cup of thick coffee from the customer lounge and came up front to the showroom. It was about 8:30 AM.

There weren't too many people, around so I went by the sales desk and just waited for the salespeople to arrive. A customer with a computer printout walked in the front door by the receptionist. There was another customer sitting by the door reading the newspaper.

I didn't see any salespeople yet so I greeted the customer. She told me that she wanted information on a particular vehicle. I said that I would get her a salesperson or help her myself.

I turned to the receptionist and asked her to page a salesperson. She immediately pointed to the "customer" that was reading the newspaper by the door and said that he was a salesperson. This is the same door from which the real customer had just entered only moments earlier. This was embarrassing and I doubt the customer bought her new car there.

Point is, without a word, the sale was killed. That salesperson's perceived uncaring attitude turned the customer off. We need to keep this in mind.

Our posture and gestures are extremely important. We need to dig deeper. What is a good posture? Posture and gestures are about how we stand or sit and interact physically with our customers.

What is a good stance? A good stance will be well balanced. Leaning on things doesn't look good. It can look lazy and uncaring. Try to stand or sit straight like our mothers told us. It's professional and makes a statement that you are interested and care about your customer.

You may also want to lean towards your customer when they are speaking and nod. This shows that you are listening. Even if you are faking it, you will actually listen more effectively. Take it from someone with a short attention span, it helps.

Other gestures are also very important. A simple handshake is not so simple. I once read this book on sales psychology, that told me that when I shook someone's hand, I should turn it so my hand was on top to show that I was in control.

I thought that it worked great until I met someone who must have read the same book. It looked like a wrestling match on the showroom floor. No, I didn't get that sale.

One of the nice things about gestures is, just as you are telling things to your customers through your gestures, they are telling you things as well. What is the customer trying to say to me by grasping my hand and squeezing it hard or turning it so their hand is on top?

They are trying to tell me that they wish to be in control. Why do they want to be in control so badly? Maybe because they are afraid and or somewhat insecure about the situation.

And what if I let them squeeze my hand? Big deal. I now know how to better approach this person.

What's the right type of handshake? In our western society, our hand would be straight up on its side. The grip would be firm and the handshake would last but a moment. This goes when shaking a man or woman's hand.

However, you need to keep in mind that there can be many cultural differences in our country and many different beliefs. Would you say it's okay to shake everyone's hand?

Think about this for a second. Would you shake a Muslim woman's hand? Unless they are fully westernized I would not. What about in Latin culture? What about other various religions? It gets complicated.

Use common sense and your best guess. Also, ask friends and workers with different backgrounds about this. If you find out now it will save deals later.

Use appropriate gestures. Open palms, no clenched fist, keep your shoulders straight, and no obscene gestures! Think about your own body language and pay attention to your customers! It's a wealth of knowledge.

Facial Expressions and Eye Contact

What's the saying? "Eyes are the windows to the soul." It is so true and if people don't look you in the eye when they speak with you, chances are that you know something's up.

What do you think is going on when your young son tells you that he didn't break the vase, and he won't look you in the eye? You would perceive that he is lying, and you would probably be right.

If your spouse is speaking with you, and you just go, "Uh huh," what will she think? That you don't care and in actuality, she's right. Remember to fake it until you make it. I'm sure that I'm not alone with this one.

This is not the best time to tell them that they are lying either. Letting your customer save face is something we'd better get used to. In most cases, they won't swallow their pride, they'll just come up with an excuse to leave and buy somewhere else.

This is the same thing that Jim from the PDA service department did with me. He knew that I was lying about my PDA. He didn't call me a liar, he just let me say that I made a mistake when I grabbed the wrong charger. I still paid to have the PDA fixed. He still got the sale and closed the deal. Let your customers save face!

Ask yourself, what happens when you look and smile at someone? Most people will smile right back at you. Let me get this straight. I smile, they smile and it affects their attitude? Could this help me make a deal? How about that?

Start becoming aware of your facial expressions. Do you really think that frowning, chewing with your mouth open or winking every two seconds at the customer's spouse is an effective technique in closing a sale? Some might interpret these gestures or habits the wrong way, and they can be irritating. Be aware of what your non-verbals are saying!

Verbal Communication

Verbal is just what it sounds like. It's about the words we use and the tone and inflection of our voice. They are very important, but the visual cues that we discussed earlier are more so.

The way we articulate things can be an art. Some of our recent presidents are very good at it and are at this moment, working with other politicians, trying to get all the money that we earn.

57

Most likely to save some soon to be extinct pesky insect in the Alaskan wilderness to get favor with an environmental activist group of some kind, but that's a story for another writer. We need to use our voice and articulate better.

Try this out. I've bolded and underlined different words in the same sentence below. Emphasize these selected words when you read each statement. Think about how the different emphasis changes the meaning of the sentence.

<u>How</u> will you be enjoying this new stainless steel Weber grill?
How will **<u>you</u>** be enjoying this **<u>new</u>** stainless steel Weber grill?
How will you be **<u>enjoying</u>** this **<u>new stainless steel</u>** Weber grill?
How will **<u>you</u>** be **<u>enjoying</u>** this **<u>new stainless steel Weber</u>** grill?

What do you think? By emphasizing different words and articulating differently you can add value to the statement differently. Depending on what was most important to the customer you can use the best incarnation of this statement to increase the value and impact of this statement.

Have statements prepared. Preparation is one of the keys to success. Come up with statements that fit your product or service.

And there is no reason not to be prepared. Most companies have training and material, which will pretty much give you what you need. There are all kinds of books on the shelf that can help you. You just need to do some work, take the material, and tweak it to make it work for you. It's the same thing with ideas from this book.

Listening

We've discussed the way we talk, what about when our customers talk? What do we need to do? We need to listen. I mean to really listen. You've heard the expression that God gave us all two ears and one mouth, so we could listen more. It's true.

In the end of this remember what we are trying to do. We are trying to get information, so we can sell something. We can't do that if we don't listen to our customers. How many of us have talked ourselves out of a sale?

Listening isn't easy and I know because I have very difficult time doing it. My problem is sometimes when something is said, my mind may run off with it into another world in a place far, far away.

I don't know how many people have this problem, but it's very embarrassing when you come out of hyper-space, and you hear someone asking you what you think, and you have to ask what the question was in the first place. It's not good for a career either.

Let's call this active listening. Use your body language to help you. Lean forward to your customer and nod as you soak it in. Ask to take notes if necessary.

This is all easy in theory, but it takes work to maintain and develop any relationship. You'll also find that when you show that you are listening, most people will respond in kind. They might give you more information and that's a good thing. Show that you are listening and it will show the customer that you care.

Develop and use good communication skills, it's not easy, but it is common sense.

- Tip 29. Be aware of verbal and non-verbal communication.
- Tip 30. Know how to communicate in a positive manner.
- Tip 31. Show you are listening and it shows that you care.

"Two monologues do not
make a dialogue."

- *Anonymous*

Chapter 7: Offer an Awesome Experience

A few years ago, my family and I took a trip to *Disney World* in Orlando, Florida. We stayed at the *Wilderness Lodge*, which has a *Yellowstone Park* type of theme. It was a scene right from a *Yogi Bear* cartoon.

We went to dinner one night in the lodge and the price for dinner was about 24 dollars a head at the time. I would certainly eat enough to get my money's worth, but I wasn't sure that my daughter, Kirstie three years old at the time, would. In the menu, there was a disclaimer that children under three would eat for free. I like free.

Well, my daughter was certainly not going to eat 24 dollars worth of food. Candy and sweets maybe, but real food, no. After moaning about it for a while, I finally got around to ask the server about the charge for my young daughter.

So what if the kids had a great time running around the restaurant in a make believe round up while we were there? So what if it was all I could eat? What about my money? What about me?

It only took a second for him to respond with, "Don't worry about it sir. I'll take it off the bill. We want your stay to be magical!"

Boy, did he make me mad. I had all that energy built up so I could vent on the guy, and he left me there with my mouth hanging open. I was so upset by what he did, that immediately after dinner, I went into the gift shop and bought two hundred dollars in *Disney* toys and coffee mugs. I showed him!

Do you think *Disney* knows this? Absolutely, I tried the same routine in other restaurants in the park and they all said the same thing, "Don't worry about it sir. I'll take it off the bill. We want your stay to be magical!" I guess that I'm not the only one buying *Disney* toys and mugs. What an experience!

One other experience that I would like to share with you about *Disney* is when we visited again in spring of 2005. It was my daughter's birthday, and we were going to eat the dinner buffet at the *Boma* restaurant in the *African Lodge*.

I mentioned to the hostess that it was my daughter's birthday. I knew that they would probably do something, and I wanted to make it nice, for my daughter, so I brought it up.

Well, they didn't take her dinner off my bill, but they did make it magical. My daughter was served a small jelly-bean decorated cake in the shape of a *Mickey Mouse* head with a candle.

Many restaurants will serve a small cake or cupcake gratis to the birthday girl. However, no other restaurant I know gives the birthday girl a card signed by most of the wait staff in their native tongues wishing her a happy birthday.

It was cute and my daughter loved it. It's just a thought, but do you think that someone ran around with a card when we were there and had all of their servers sign it or do you think that they had a stack of cards already signed and ready to go?

Maybe they just needed to write in my daughter's name. You can mull that over for a few minutes, but it sounds like a process to me.

Pretty impressive and awesome, wouldn't you say? By the way, a birthday card with an autographed picture of *Snow White and the Seven Dwarfs* was also put in our room while we were out for the day. Kudos *Disney!*

I'll suggest at this point to somehow make a note of when you had an awesome experience and what was done. You might be able to take their idea and apply it to your business. That's called innovation. There are a couple of lined pages in the back of the book for you to write them down.

Look around you! Who else do you know, offers a great experience? Ever rent a car from *Enterprise*? Travel on *Southwest Airlines*? Buy something in *Nordstrom?* All of them are strong on having processes for their procedures.

I'm not saying they're perfect, but overall they offer better experiences for their customers than their competition. Look to outfits like them for ideas.

You can spend an unbelievable amount of money on a customer experience and still have it fail. It's not really like *Field of Dreams,* "If you build it, they will come." Even *Disney* had problems in France with *Euro Disney* for a while, because the experience in Europe needed to be different. They made their adjustments and offer a great experience in *Euro Disney*, it's just different from the one that you get in the states.

You may not have to spend a lot to offer a great experience for your customers. Given, some higher ticket items might justify it. Free maintenance in the case of *BMW* or free suites for those extremely high rollers in Las Vegas. How about a great test drive or product demonstration? People like free.

The company needs to take care of higher dollar items. However, what can we do on an individual basis? There are things that guys like us can do.

Cheap:

1. Create a good business card that separates you from others.
2. Give-a-ways for their kids to play with.
3. Are refreshments available for your customers?
4. Mints available?
5. Do you have everything handy to complete orders?
6. Take photos of customers and their new car? Or boat?

Hopefully, a few of these ideas will get your gears turning.

Free:

1. Remember your appearance! Be clean and professional.
2. Smile a lot, it's contagious.
3. Follow a professional process, show you know what you're doing.
4. Learn and be an expert on your product or service.
5. Relieve your customer's stress, let them buy.
6. Offer a great presentation.
7. Get them the information they need.

I guess most of the ideas that help make a great experience don't require money. Go figure? What are your ideas? Be creative and separate yourself from others! Make it special!

Don't worry, you'll get to implement this information in the practical application section.

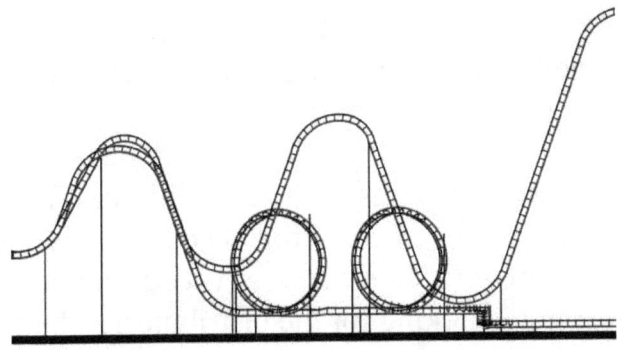

- Tip 32: Take note of your awesome experiences.
- Tip 33: Innovate and use other experiences to create one for your customers.
- Tip 34: You don't have to spend a lot to offer a great experience.
- Tip 35: Separate yourself from others by the experience that you offer.

"A great sales process will not only lead to sales, it will also lead to a great experience for your customers."

- Rip Walker

Chapter 8: Focus on Your Customer

Many companies use surveys to measure customer satisfaction. Many model ones after the *J. D. Power and Associates* survey. They survey just about everything.

In any case, *Toyota* uses surveys modeled after *J. D. Power*. The score can sometimes affect various incentives to dealers and staff. If you don't have the right score, you don't get your incentive money.

My friend, another car salesperson, had an issue. His Sales Person Index (SPI) score wasn't high enough for him to qualify for his salesperson incentives. It was costing him buckets of money. I was now working for the distributor, so he called me and asked for help.

I spoke with him and suggested that we take a look at some of his surveys and see what comments his customers were making. We did and we found a pattern.

My friend is a great guy, so I figured that it was something simple. Reading through the surveys the pattern was that people did not feel that he was considerate of their time.

He sells over 400 vehicles a year, which is awesome and outstanding. He is one of *Toyota's* top salespeople. Most of his business is made up of repeat and referral sales.

By the way, these types of sales are more profitable than new customer sales. At times he would have five people in the dealership showroom waiting for him.

Here's where the problem was, he would be sitting with one customer while at the same time looking out the corner of his eye at another customer.

It's kind of like my spouse trying to talk to me while I'm watching *24* on television. For those of you who haven't watched this, it's one of those addictive action shows.

In any case, could my spouse tell that I wasn't listening? Would she say that I'm not being considerate of her time? How about my friend's customers? How did they feel?

Here was our solution, be there for your customers. In other words, be there mentally and not just physically. If you can't be there mentally, it would be better to tell them so. It's easier said than done.

Focusing on your customer is a key to a great experience. With all the distractions that we have these days, how do we keep our attention on our customer?

You can include things in your process to help you. Aside from the notes on listening, which we talked about earlier, here are a few rules about focusing to go by.

Rip's Rules of Customer Focus:

1. Do not take phone calls when you are with a customer.

   Turn your cell phone off during interaction with your customer. Think how you feel when someone that you are speaking with takes a phone call and cuts you off. The statement, "I have to take this call," doesn't do anything for me, and I'll walk out of the store. Getting paged doesn't help either.

How about this, I turn off my cell phone in front of the customer and call the receptionist and tell her to hold my calls. What did I just say to my customer? I told them that I care and that this person in front of me is more important than anyone else. There's not too many people out there who do this. An action like this will separate you from others.

2. Other distractions should be eliminated if possible.

   Is there television on behind you? Is someone's music too loud? Smoke coming in? Another salespeople talking too loud near you? All of these can kill a sale.

   Do something like we mentioned before. Turn down the noise and ask other salespeople to move their conversations elsewhere. Your customers will appreciate the gesture.

3. There should be nothing distracting about you.

   We talked about appearance and body language earlier. Is there anything on your person that would be distracting?

   I'm not saying that the *Tweety Bird* tie is too much, but maybe the blinking of your cell phone in your pocket might bother people. What about your breath?

   Any bad habits that get on a person's nerves? Ever have a person who winks at you after they think they've said something cute and witty? Drives me nuts. Hey, we all have our twitches, but be aware of them and try to put them to rest.

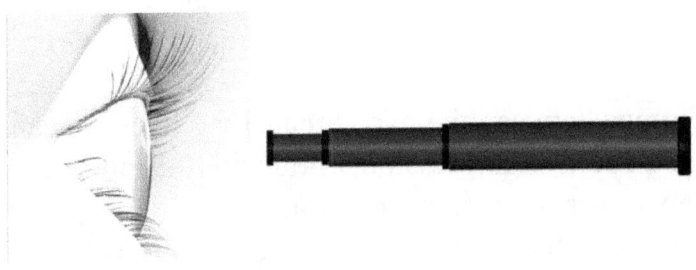

- Tip 36: Listen and focus on your customer.
- Tip 37: Don't take calls when with a customer.
- Tip 38:. Eliminate distractions.
- Tip 39: Make sure that you are not the distraction.

"With customers, mentally being there shows that you care."

- Rip Walker

Chapter 9: Make a Great First and Last Impression

First and last impressions are two of the most important parts of a sales process. Your first impression may kill the sale from the get go while a bad last impression will certainly kill future sales.

The difference between the two is that sometimes we can overcome a bad first impression while with the latter we will most likely never see that customer again. All of us experienced salespeople have had this happen to us.

The First Impression

This brings to mind something that happened to me a few years ago. See if something like this has happened to you. I went with one of our District Sales Managers on a joint client visit in southern Georgia. We were to visit the father and son owners of one of our distributor's stores. Now being somewhat new in the field, I did not use common sense.

In any case, we go into the store, speak with dad, and then we take the son out to lunch. The son is dressed in jeans and a sport shirt. He was in his early to late twenties. Here I went again, judging a book by its cover.

Once at the restaurant, I took the opportunity to immediately raise both of my feet and shove them into my mouth. I said, "So you're the dealer's son?" I figured that I had been a dealer's son, and I will now build rapport, by talking about something that we have in common. I continued and asked, "What's your dad got you doing?" He hardly said a word to me over lunch and through the rest of the visit.

I got a call from the District Sales Manager the next afternoon, and he tells me that he spoke with our friend from lunch and was asked, "What did he do to me?"

I had insulted him tremendously. He was the General Manager of the store. Yes, he was young and I made a mistake. I made a bad impression by not being prepared. It took me a year to fix that one. Too many of these will just kill you.

What can we to do to make a good impression? What would be common sense?

Be prepared and do your research! Find out who they are. Find out what they do. Find out everything that you can about your prospective customer. What they like and what they don't like. What are their pet peeves? What are their hobbies? Married? Kids? What are they proud of?

Is there anything that you shouldn't talk about? There are good reasons why you should avoid talking about religion or politics. Most people have strong beliefs about either one, and they are typically emotionally charged!

If you're lucky, maybe the previous representative can fill you in on clients that they are familiar with. Look for cues from the customer as well. Their favorite team logo might be right on their baseball cap. The more that you know, the better off that you'll be.

You also have to look at your own personnel attitude and the image that is projected from the way you dress.

Let's talk about the image thing first, because it's usually easier to change. It's not necessarily cheaper, but easier.

As they say, take a look in the mirror. Look at your appearance. Are you well groomed? No food in your beard? No hair creeping out of your nose or ears? (That's for the over 40 crowd.) There is simply no reason for not being well groomed at least at the start of the day.

Actually, with modern technology there is probably no reason for not being well groomed at the end of the day as well. Bring an electric razor, a change of clothes, a tooth brush, mouth wash, etc. Yes, it's a pain, but it will do wonders.

Just think how someone feels when they speak with you after you've had onion soup for lunch. I love it too, but I avoid these things when I'm going to be face to face with someone.

Let's talk about attitude. There have been more books and courses than we can count about how our attitude affects us and everything we do. Attitude is the most important part of selling.

Say you had a bad day, what are you going to do? Sometimes there is not much you can do except to try and get away from everyone else and ride it out. Take time off, take a walk, etc. This will help your future prospects and relationships.

A few years ago my older brother died unexpectedly. I received the news of my brother's death while watching *OJ Simpson* and his *Bronco* on TV. I was a mess and I cried all night and didn't sleep.

The funeral was to be in a few days. I decided to go to work to help get my mind off of his death. It might have been a good idea if I worked in a corner office somewhere where I could close the door and disappear, but I was an Assistant Manager at a car dealership and would be in face to face contact with customers and salespeople.

A stupid thought crossed my mind on the way in, "Maybe customers will feel sorry for me and buy cars?" The truth is that they felt very uncomfortable and wanted to leave as quickly as possible.

My breakdowns during the day didn't help. I told people my allergies were acting up. I don't think that they believed me. The General Manager finally asked me to leave for the day. I didn't close any sales that day and I surely didn't look in the mirror that morning.

Try not to beat yourself up too much. Things sometimes just happen. Here are some ideas, which you can use to make a great first impression:

Cheap:

1. Unique business cards.
2. Personal hygiene kit that includes mouthwash.
3. Dress sharp.
4. Prepared material.
5. Candy and mints on your desk.

Free:

1. Exhibit your professionalism at all times.
2. Find as much as you can about your customer.
3. Carry an awesome attitude.
4. Have a sense of humor.
5. Smile and relax.

What are some things that you can do to help make a great 1st impression?

Things to make a great first impression:

1. _____
   _____

2. _____
   _____

3. _____
   _____

4. _____
   _____

5. _____
   _____

If you don't have too much at this point, give it some time. You'll come up with something. Onto the last impression.

Hi!

- Tip 40: As earlier, offer a great appearance.
- Tip 41: Do your homework and research about your customer.
- Tip 42: Have a great attitude.
- Tip 43: Don't bring your personal problems in with you.
- Tip 44: Don't beat yourself up too much.

"You never get a second chance to make a first impression."

- Anonymous

The Last Impression

Nordstrom is one of the most successful chains of department stores in the world. They are upscale, typically charge more for their wares than other department stores, and they are profitable. And they have one of the highest customer satisfaction ratings in the business. How do they do it?

There are many reasons, but what I'd ask you to notice is the next time you shop in a *Nordstrom* store, pay attention to how the salesperson finishes your purchase. They will always ask or suggest something to go with an outfit or article of clothing.

They will also, come out from behind the counter to hand you the purchased items. This policy is trained and monitored for accountability.

This is the last part of their sales process that the *Nordstrom* sales consultant does with their customers after consummating a sale, aside from some follow up notes they sometimes send. What does this do for the customer and the sales consultant?

It makes a great last impression with their customers. A great last impression is almost as important as a great first impression. This is because the last impression is what they will be most likely to remember, and it will be a major reason for them to come back.

Their last experience, is one that the customer will most likely use to decide if they will purchase from you again. It builds the relationship between the sales consultant, the store, and the customer. Don't forget it! Its common sense.

What can you do to make an awesome last impression that customers will remember you for and come back to you? Here are a few examples, which won't cost you a dime.

Free:

1. Again, Exhibit your professionalism at all times

2. Carry an awesome attitude.
3. Answer any questions about their purchase.
4. Thank them for coming by or allowing your visit.
5. Make sure that they know how their purchase operates.
6. Set up a follow up to ensure their satisfaction.

What are some things that you can do to help make a great last impression?

1. _____

_____

2. _____

_____

3. _____

_____

4. _____

_____

5. _____

_____

Be creative with ideas. You don't have to break the bank to create a great experience. Take a few ideas and innovate, and you can get your customers to remember you.

- Tip 45: Make it special!
- Tip 46: Have a great attitude during the entire process.
- Tip 47: Treat your customers like gold.
- Tip 48: Appreciate their purchase and let them know.

"You're only as good
as your last impression."

- *Rip Walker*

Section II: Theory in Your Process – Practical Application

Now that you have all of this theory, it's time to take some action. Many books will give you all the warm and fuzzy theory, but this one will help you put theory into an application.

Theories are wonderful, but as my father would say, "Wishing for it, ain't going to make it happen." It's good to be optimistic, but you and I are responsible for making things happen.

If you plan on becoming successful in any business or endeavor, you are ultimately responsible. Yes, there can be set backs like an economic downturn, but you can either sit and complain or make something happen.

In my case, I was laid off in March of 2009. I had been with *Southeast Toyota Distributors, LLC* for over 14 years. I did a good job, and I was a good employee, but things happen, and it wasn't my fault.

I am the one responsible for my future, so I decided to go out as an independent business consultant. I would consult, train, and write books for my living. Nothing like knowing that your money will run out to give you that extra motivation.

I'm a sales subject matter expert, I can speak in public, and I can train. What is your position? What can you do? What are you an expert at? We all need to take responsibility and make the effort to try and succeed.

Over this section, we'll take you through a template that you can use to build your awesome sales process. Keep in mind that you can make it as long as you want or as in depth.

Most processes are works in progress that continually need improving. *Toyota* uses the Japanese word *Kaizen*, which means continuous improvement. It's time to improve, *Kaizen*!

THEORY
+ APPLICATION

= ACTION

- Tip 49: Take action.
- Tip 50: You are responsible for your life.

- Tip 51: Make an effort to succeed.

"Wishing for it, ain't going to make it happen."

- William J. Walker

Chapter 10: First Impression – What's Your Process?

Keeping in mind what you have learned so far, what are your goals that you wish to achieve during your initial contact with your customer?

I'll give you some suggestions, but you have to make the final decision. I understand that it's tough, but it is your process.

Goals

Some possible goals, at first contact, to achieve a great first impression could be to:

1. Have the customer start to relax.
2. Have them start liking me.
3. Have them start to trust me.
4. Get them to follow my process.
5. Get them to interact with me.

What do you want to achieve? What are your goals for this part of your process?

1. _____
2. _____
3. _____

4. _____
5. _____

How Will These Goals Be Reached?

You now know what you would like to achieve in this part of the process. How are you going to achieve your goals? Let's think this through.

You're going to have to greet your customer somewhere aren't you? Where will it be? Will it be in a showroom, an office, or in a house? It gets a little more complicated doesn't it?

Keep in mind what your goals are and where you want to go next. Do you want them to sit at your desk with you? Do you wish to have them let you in their home?

Where will I greet my customer? What will I do? What will I say?

_____
_____

Why am I doing it this way?

_____
_____

Am I doing anything to make it special to make it a better experience for my customer?

_____

_____

You've decided where and what will you say. Maybe it's something like, "Welcome to the ABC Store! I'm Rip Walker and you are?" Write your greeting below.

My greeting:

_____

_____

Why am I doing it this way?

_____

_____

Make it special?

_____

_____

Hopefully, you've kept in mind all the things we covered in the book and will include something special for your customers.

At this point, we will be transitioning into our next part of the process, but how do we get there? You need to use some kind of transitional statement. Usually a question of some kind.

Please, remember this statement, "He or she who asks the questions is in control." I don't believe that you can actually control someone, because if they really want to they can walk out of your store or ask you to leave. But, with good questions, you can guide them. Usually it helps to offer a benefit to them.

At one store, I used to call on they had a monthly flat screen television give-away. The receptionist would ask customers as they entered the building, "Would you like to enter our monthly drawing? We just need to step inside." It worked pretty well, or how about, "I'd really like to get you some information, but it would be better to sit at my desk for few moments to get it for you." Or, "The washer and dryer that you are looking for is in another section. Please, follow me."

What is your transitional statement? What will you say to get the customer to follow your process? By the way, don't get too frustrated if they won't follow you. It happens sometimes.

My transitional statement:

_____

_____

Why did I ask this?

_____

_____

Most likely you will be moving into some type of fact finding process. A process where you want to find out the customer's needs and wants. Let's go on to our next chapter and put a discovery process together.

- Tip 52: Create goals for each part of your process.
- Tip 53: Write out the what and why of your process.
- Tip 54: Use transitional statements or questions to move through your process.

"He or she who asks the questions is in control."

- Rip Walker

Chapter 11: Discovering Wants and Needs – What to Ask?

Goals

What are your goals that you wish to achieve during this part of the process? Here are a few suggestions, but again, you have to make the decision. Use goals that would be appropriate in your business, mine may not apply.

Some possible goals to achieve during this part of the process might be...

1. Continue to have the customer relax.
2. To gather information about your customer's wants and needs.
3. To continue to move through the process smoothly.
4. To build more rapport with your customer.
5. To gain more trust.

What do you want to achieve?

1. _____
2. _____
3. _____
4. _____

5. _____

You can add more goals if your sales process dictates that you do. As it was covered earlier, your process might be very short, and maybe it doesn't even require much in the way of discovery. You decide, but let's continue.

Questions

I'm going to share some general discovery questions with you to help get you to brainstorm your own. You know what you need to find out so alter or disregard the questions that I give you.

Most will be open, because we want to gain as much information that we can while at the same time allowing our customer to relax. Below are examples of "Starter Questions."

Starter Questions

- What brought you here today?

- How familiar are you with ABC product or service?

- What are you looking for in your new dryer, or Car?

- Describe for me what you hope that this new camera… bicycle… watch… will do for you?

- What's most important to you in selecting a new…house? TV? Computer?

Even though these are open questions your customer may respond with a closed answer. If I ask a customer what features would you like in your new car, they may say that they want it loaded.

What does "loaded" mean? It will mean different things to different people. Common sense tells us that we need more information so that means we have to ask another question to have them expand on what they've given us. Here are what I call, "Expanding Questions."

Expanding Questions

- Tell me more?

- Why do you say that?

- What do you mean?

- For example?

- What else should I know?

Remember your body language and gestures when you ask questions. You want them to keep giving you information, so look them in the eye and keep nodding your head. And take notes! You'll be surprised at what a customer will let you know when they realize that you are sincerely paying attention.

Put yourself in the customer's shoes. Many people don't get this kind of attention at home.

The customer has now given you all the information that you need to continue right? Are you sure? How can you find out if you got it all? You need to ask another question or make a statement that will allow the customer to give you specific information that will help you guide the sales process.

I'm calling these, "Confirming Statements." When you use them a customer will either confirm, correct, or add to the information. The directions are simple, start the statement and then repeat information that they told you.

Confirming Statements

- So what you're saying is…(You want a four door, with leather and an automatic transmission.)

- If I understand you correctly…(You would like a house with three bedrooms and hardwood floors.)

- Let me see if I have this right…(You told me that you need your belongings delivered by June 23rd?)

By repeating the information you get to make sure that you have gotten it right. The customer feels that you listen and care. And as I said, if you got it wrong, you've allowed the customer to come back and give you more information so you can make a better recommendation.

I've put in some blanks below for you to insert your questions. Please, customize your questions to your sales process and remember to write in the **"Why"** below it. This will help you focus on what you need to ask and not just ask questions for the sake of asking questions.

Remember your goals for this part of the process. We need to be efficient throughout the process to make it a great experience.

Don't forget the theory behind your process and is there anything special that you wish to include into your process? It's okay if you don't have something special to do at each question, but if you think of something, write it down.

What are your *Starter Questions*?

1. _____
   _____

   Why am I asking this question?
   _____
   _____

   Make it special?
   _____
   _____

2. _____
   _____

Why am I asking this question?

_____

_____

Make it special?

_____

_____

3. _____

_____

Why am I asking this question?

_____

_____

Make it special?

_____

_____

4. _____

_____

Why am I asking this question?

_____

_____

Make it special?

_____

_____

5. _____

_____

Why am I asking this question?

_____

_____

Make it special?

_____

_____

What are your *Expanding Questions*?

The reason why you ask these questions is to get more information. If your reason is different, then write it down.

1. _____

_____

Why am I asking this question?

_____

_____

Make it special?

_____

_____

2. _____

_____

Why am I asking this question?

_____

_____

Make it special?

_____

_____

3. _____

_____

Why am I asking this question?

_____

_____

Make it special?

_____

_____

4. _____

_____

Why am I asking this question?

_____

_____

Make it special?

_____

_____

5. _____

_____

Why am I asking this question?

_____

_____

Make it special?

_____

_____

What are your *Confirming Statements*?

A confirming statement is used to verify the information that you received from your customer.

Check this out, what is your customer saying when you repeat back the information, and you get it right? They say yes! Could that be a close?

1. _____

_____

Why am I asking this question?

_____

_____

Make it special?

_____

_____

2. _____

_____

Why am I asking this question?

_____

_____

Make it special?

_____

_____

3. _____

_____

Why am I asking this question?

_____

_____

Make it special?

_____

_____

Closing happens throughout the process, not only when you present numbers. At this stage in your process, they should be closed on what a caring, nice salesperson you are. We have more to go here to fully develop your process.

- Tip 55: I repeat, create goals for each part of your process.
- Tip 56: Use Starter Questions, Expanding Questions, and Confirming Statements.

- Tip 57: Closing happens throughout the sales process.

"To get the right answers,
you need to ask the right questions."

- *Rip Walker*

Chapter 12: How Will You Make Your Recommendation?

I recently married a wonderful woman who loves and cares for me a great deal. I would die for her, and I mean that. Don't marry someone who wouldn't do the same for you. Trust me.

In any case, I went into a *Jared* jewelry store to buy a diamond engagement ring for my new bride. I had been dealing with a really intelligent, professional salesperson who I had purchased a watch from a few months earlier. I trust and like the guy. Not pushy, very knowledgeable, and just a good guy.

I was hemming and hawing about a ring for my wife. It was expensive, but I wanted it for my wife, and I was ready to do something. Whatever money I had was burning a nice hole in my right front pants pocket.

The ring was a thousand dollars more than I wanted to spend. The salesperson made a fine recommendation to close the deal. He held out two settings, and he asked me to see if I could tell the difference. I said no, that I couldn't.

He then told me that one was platinum and one was white gold. The white gold would save me the thousand dollars that I needed.

I liked the idea and he said if my wife didn't like the setting, we could exchange it without a problem. He was right, my loving wife was fine with the purchase.

He closed the deal, because he made a recommendation. He didn't lower his price, and he didn't give away profit. He used common sense, made a recommendation, and gave me an option.

How do you actually set this recommendation up? If you've done a good job getting and analyzing your customer's information it's not a problem.

Unfortunately, many salespeople don't do the work or get really nervous about losing the sale. They might say to themselves, " What will the customer think if I do this? Maybe they'll get up and walk out."

This is letting fear make our decisions. Get the knowledge, reduce your fear, and be brave. And you can always drop the price. A professional will try to keep gross in the deal and exhaust a few means before discounting.

Once you have the information it's a simple case of presenting the options. The nice thing about options is that they are choices. You might still get a "no," but you might get the customer to make a choice and make the sale for you.

It could go something like this…

Salesperson: Rip, I know that you really want the platinum setting?

Rip: Yes.

Salesperson: And it's just pushing you over your budget?

Rip: Yes.

Salesperson: Could I show you something that might save you the money to get the ring that you want?

Rip: Yes.

The salesperson places two identical settings onto the display fabric for me to see. He hands me a loop. (At least I thought they were identical.)

Salesperson: Take a close look please.

I took a close look at the two. He waits a few seconds.

Salesperson: Would you like to know what the difference is between the two?

Rip: Yes?

Salesperson: The one on the left is $1200 dollars less.

Rip: Really?

Salesperson: It's a white gold setting, and it's $1200 less. You can't tell the difference. And knowing your wife, she would probably be okay with it. If she isn't we can take the ring back, or you can change the setting when you can afford it.

Rip: Mmmm…

Salesperson: I'll take that as a yes?

In any case, he closed the deal. And we did end up changing the setting later. Point is, he closed the deal and took me out of the market for a ring.

Let's examine what he did. First, he had a lot of information. I was a returning customer, and he had a good relationship with me. The trust was there. This allows him to be "stronger" with me.

What I mean is that he could be much more at ease in asking questions and trying to close me on the sale.

Second, he also knew my wife pretty well and knew her probable reactions.

Third, he thought everything out and made his recommendations, and yes he asked for the sale again.

There's some information on closing here, but we'll get deeper into that in a bit. By using common sense, he made the deal.

Unfortunately most salespeople just take a customer's word for what they want to buy and never use the information that they have to make a recommendation. Let me give you an example.

A couple comes in and they say they want to buy the fully equipped $40,000 top of the line *Toyota Avalon*. They tell you they know what they want. You say okay. You ask a few questions, you disregard the facts that they don't have the income, the down payment, or the credit to buy this car. And never mind that they pulled up in a worn out 1982 *Oldsmobile Cutlass*.

You build some rapport, offer a great presentation, and you apply all the great theory that was described earlier in this book. You've given them a demonstration drive and built value in you and your place of business. You and your customers are having a great time.

You all sit down in your office a bit later. Refreshments are out and it will just take a minute to get them the numbers, and then you can wrap this up.

In your mind, you've already bought the new 50" HD flat screen with your commission, and you are watching your local professional football team in larger than life color.

You return to your desk with a big smile. You've already taken the liberty of filling out the buyer's order. The customers look at the numbers in front of them. Their smiles suddenly fade away.

So does yours as they ask if there is anything you can do on the price. You run back and forth to the sales desk a few times. Your sales manager isn't too happy either.

Finally there's a turn from a sales manager. He asks your customers a few questions, then the customers get up, tell you that they will think about it, and they walk out the door. Just as they get into their car, they remark that you are a great salesperson.

You wonder the rest of the day why they didn't buy. "They told me that's what they wanted," you say to yourself. You feel pretty bad so you decide to pick up a frozen latte of some kind at the local coffee shop on the way home to watch the football game on your old *Zenith* 19".

When you go to park by the coffee shop, you notice that there's a brand new economy sedan parked out front with a temp tag on it. You walk into the shop and there are your *Avalon* customers sipping on frozen drinks.

The customers turn and they remember you. They immediately tell you that they got a better deal. That really makes you feel good. Even so, a better deal on what? The car they bought isn't close to an *Avalon*. It's $20,000 less! What happened?

Most people will walk into a place wanting one thing and buying something else. It doesn't matter what you're selling, people change their minds all the time.

Making a recommendation is what professionals do. That's why they make more money. In this past story, if the customer actually bought the Avalon, the deal wouldn't have had much profit. There is a saying, "The happiest customers are the ones that you made the most money on."

Typically, the customers that you made the least money on never saw the value in what they bought and will always think that you made too much.

These customers saw more value in the other car. It's all perceptions, but because the salesperson didn't make a recommendation of a lesser vehicle to the customer, he lost the sale all together. Let's look into how to make a recommendation.

Steps to a Recommendation

1. Gather customer information prior to making the recommendation and verify that the information is correct. This step overlaps with the discovery part of your process.

2. Think about what will actually fit into your customer's needs. This is where you earn your pay. Think of it like a doctor giving a diagnosis. Screw it up and you may kill the patient.

3. Be brave and recommend what you think is the right product for them and why, even if it's not

what they told you they said that they wanted. If you want to make more money then you have to do this step!

4. Allow the customer to give you feedback that might change your recommendation. There is a possibility that you missed something.

   I was working in a *Cadillac* store years ago, when a sloppily dressed man walked in. He told the salesperson that he wanted a *Cadillac Eldorado*.

   The salesperson asked him what he did for a living and the customer told him that he worked as a waiter.

   The salesperson recommended a used car and figured that the customer couldn't afford more and then sent the customer off.

   Three days later, there was a big picture of the customer, his new *Cadillac Eldorado,* and the salesperson from another dealer, who sold him the car. The headline said, "Local Lotto Winner Buys New *Cadillac Eldorado*."

   Get information and get feedback from your customers. You don't know everything and things change for people all the time. Who knows, maybe your customer is more qualified than you might think.

5. Continue to the next part of your process.

Here's a format for your recommendation. "A way, not the way," as my old boss and mentor Reginald Vaughn would say.

Mr. Customer, based on what you told me I'd like to recommend a: _____.

Wait and see what the customer says. If they say yes, that's great. Continue on to the next part of your process. However, what if they say no? What if they tell you they know what they want?

This is the part where many salespeople collapse and fold. If you give way, most likely you will only be able to negotiate price later.

At this point, you need to ask for the feedback and get more information. You need to step back into the discovery part and ask more questions.

Ask more expanding questions., like, "What have I missed?" "What else do I need to know?" You might find out that they have more money to buy your product. Then change your recommendation.

What if they give you more information, and it still points you to a lesser product? This is where you use your recommendation to set up a switch product or service for later when you are negotiating.

You set up alternatives later by letting them know that they may have to be more flexible to get the product or service that they want.

That might mean more cash down or flexibility on equipment and accessories or different financial arrangements. We'll discuss this when we get to closing later in the book. For now let's get this part on paper.

Here's a template to follow:

Salesperson: Mr. Customer, based on what you told me I'd like to recommend a _____.
(If the customer says yes, continue to your presentation.)

Customer: No, I want the _____.

Salesperson: Mr. Customer, from what you told me I thought that this might be a good choice. Please, tell me what I missed?

Customer: I just really want the _____.

Salesperson: We can look at that, but it will require more money down to fit it into your budget. You might have to be flexible on the options, the availability or the color.

What is your recommendation process?

_____

_____

What is your statement of recommendation?

_____

_____

What is your response when the customer says they still want the un-recommended product or service?

_____

_____

You now have a way to recommend a product or service, and you have a way to set up your alternative product or service later in the process if you need to.

We'll assume that you are going to present what you've recommended.

Forward we go!

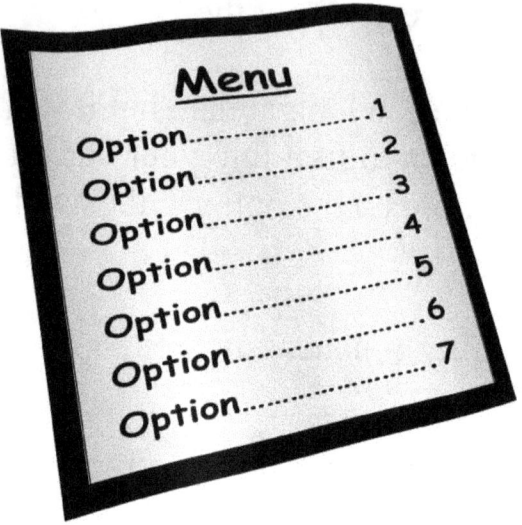

- Tip 58: Be brave and make a recommendation.
- Tip 59: Listen to customer feedback. You may have to change your recommendation.
- Tip 60: Set up alternatives and choices.

"Accomplishment is easiest when we work the hardest, and it is hardest when we work the easiest."

- *Anonymous*

Chapter 13: What is Your Process for Your Presentation?

This is another very big part of a selling process, because this is where you offer an awesome experience with what your customer will buy. This is where you build value! This is where you build gross and your commission! Don't blow it now by not being prepared. By not having a process in place! By not using common sense!

Goals

First, as always, what do you want to achieve with this part of the process? It's okay if some of your goals are the same as in a previous part of your sales process. Here are a few examples:

1. Continue to have the customer relax.
2. Build value in my product or service.
3. Continue to move through the process.
4. Continue to build more rapport with my customer.
5. To discover and overcome objections.
6. Set up my closing process

What do you want to achieve?

1. _____
2. _____
3. _____
4. _____
5. _____
6. _____

You can add more goals if your sales process dictates that you need to.

The Presentation

This is not a book where you read how to learn about your product or service. You can go to all the company training that you want to, but it's all going to come down to you.

You need to learn about what you're selling. It's not convenient and we'd all rather plunk ourselves down in front of the TV and play videos games, watch a movie, a football game, or the food channel. That's my weakness.

However, just like writing this book, nobody is going to write it for me. Grab the product book, the brochure, or go on the web, and learn about your product or service, and at the same time you might want to learn about the competition.

You're going to need this information to build your presentation and demonstration for your product or service. You are also going to need the information to handle various objections.

And you may or may not be surprised that many salespeople never really learn about what they sell and just take what gets thrown onto the wall. Some people actually make a living that way, but that's no way to really make a living.

Be a student of the business that you are in. Read your industry's publications. You never know what you might learn.

Assume that you now know your product, how is your presentation set up? Is it at someone's home, your office, a showroom? Are you selling through the web, on the phone, or in their office?

What do you need to present your product? The product itself? Video of the service? Someone to answer technical questions? A computer?

I've been at sales presentations that were quite embarrassing. One salesperson tried to sell us on some type of webcasting a few years ago. He didn't bring a computer to show us anything on the web, and he didn't have any idea about what was available on the web already.

We had already rolled out videos on the web for training salespeople and this guy was telling us that they were the only ones that could broadcast audio with pictures. He didn't know that *Yahoo* was already in the business of streaming video over the web. It wasn't a very good meeting.

In any case, write out what you need to roll out your presentation successfully on a list like the one below. Do you need the actual product? Reports? Brochures? Web access? DVDs?

What do I Need for My Presentation?

1. _____

2. _____

3. _____

4. _____

5. _____
6. _____
7. _____
8. _____
9. _____
10. _____

We have our goals and we know what we need. What about what we are going to show our customers? What about features and benefits?

In a product or service presentation, we must include features and benefits. From the information that you gathered from your customer, you should be able to present features that your customer will appreciate if you explain the benefits that specifically fit their needs and wants.

If I speak about how airbags to a twenty one year old, he'll probably fall asleep. If I show him or let him know how fast and sexy the car is, he's more likely to buy into what I'm pitching.

Don't rattle off a list of features and benefits to your customer. As a professional salesperson, try to present features and benefits that are important to your customer. If you don't, you might just be talking to yourself.

Let's put your process in writing and remember the **"Why."** Think about where you want to present features and benefits as well. Be creative, make it special and make sure that your final step is transitioning into the next part of your process.

My Process for My Presentation

Step 1: Where will I present my product? Will it be outside, inside, or on the phone?

_____

_____

      Why am I presenting it there?

      _____

      _____

      Make it special?

      _____

      _____

Step 2: What will I say or do next? Which features and benefits will I present?

_____

_____

      Why am I doing this?

      _____

      _____

      Make it special?

      _____

      _____

Step 3: What will I say or do next? Which features and benefits will I present?

_____

_____

Why am I doing this?

_____

_____

Make it special?

_____

_____

Step 4: What will I say or do next? Which features and benefits will I present?

_____

_____

Why am I doing this?

_____

_____

Make it special?

_____

_____

Step 5: What will I say or do next? Which features and benefits will I present?

_____

_____

Why am I doing this?

_____

_____

Make it special?

_____

_____

Step 6: What will I say or do next? Which features and benefits will I present?

_____

_____

Why am I doing this?

_____

_____

Make it special?

_____

_____

Step 7: What will I say or do next? Which features and benefits will I present?

_____

_____

Why am I doing this?

_____

_____

Make it special?

_____

_____

Step 8: What will I say or do next? Which features and benefits will I present?

_____

_____

      Why am I doing this?

      _____

      _____

      Make it special?

      _____

      _____

Step 9: What will I say or do next? Which features and benefits will I present?

_____

_____

      Why am I doing this?

      _____

      _____

      Make it special?

      _____

      _____

If you ran out of lines, just pick up a note pad and continue. At this point, you know how to write out a process. It's just directions.

You've sold your product and have done a great presentation. What else do you need to sell aside from your product or service? Yourself and your company. Next chapter!

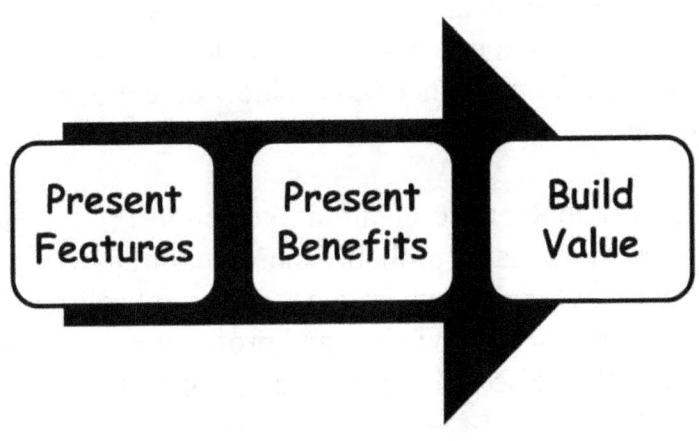

- Tip 61: Practice and prepare your presentation.
- Tip 62: Make sure that you have everything that you need.
- Tip 63: Present features and benefits that are important to the customer.

"Life itself is a matter of salesmanship"

- *Thomas J. Watson*

Chapter 14: Selling Yourself and Your Business

Somewhere in your process you need to sell yourself. Let's dedicate some time and space to help you develop a process for selling yourself and your business or company which you work for or own. It's still a process, but it would be what I would call a mini-process. You will need to decide where it belongs in your sales process.

It's really just another presentation like you just built, but your selling something that is probably more important to making the sale than the product or service that you are selling. Your appearance, product knowledge, and professionalism are a given here. What else can you offer a customer that no one else can?

That would be you of course and your place of business. Even if there is another of the same franchise down the street or across town selling the same product or service you are still unique and have things to offer that others can't.

Maybe your store has longer hours? It's a nicer facility? Better coffee in the customer lounge? Shuttle service? Free estimates? Better quality ratings?

Show the customer what you have. What can you and or your store offer? And let me give you a clue, most salespeople don't even sell themselves or their place of business.

It works like this, if you mention something of value that the other salesperson doesn't, the customer will perceive that you have it, and they don't. I lost a sale in the moving business that way.

The customer said that the other outfit was a family owned business. So was the company that I was working for, I just didn't mention it and lost the sale. Losing sales like this gets expensive over time so be smart and know what you have and share this type of information with your customer.

List out some things that might be unique about you and might be of value to your customer. I'll give you a few examples.

Do you belong to a charitable group or coach a little league team? Are you certified in your business? How long have you been in the business? Get the idea?

What's Special About You?

1. _____
2. _____
3. _____
4. _____
5. _____

List out a few things that make your company different than others. What can the company offer?

We've been in business for over 25 years. We are a member of a local charitable organization. We have a highly rated service department. We've received awards. We are recognized in the city and on and on.

What's Special About Your Company?

1. _____
2. _____
3. _____
4. _____
5. _____

If your list is too short, ask the owner and other personnel where you work. If no one can come up with something, you might have a problem.

You should now have a list of things to talk about or present, but where is the best place in your process for this part? It depends on what you are selling, but you still need to think this out. I've listed examples below.

What is the attribute? Where and when will I present this quality attribute about me or my business?

I will present our service award by the shop, before going to my desk.

    a. Why am I doing this here and why now?

       Because that's a convenient place to introduce them to service personnel, it creates a convenient flow back to my desk, and the next part of the process .

What is the attribute? Where and when will I present this quality attribute about me or my business?

<u>I will present my certifications at my desk after the product presentation.</u>

    a. Why am I doing this here and why now?

       <u>Because I've sold the product and now would be a convenient time to build value in myself and my store.</u>

Get the idea? You should be getting the hang of this. You're on your way to becoming a professional that knows what you do and why you do it that way.

Here are some blanks so you can write in your own process.

What is the attribute? Where and when will I present this quality attribute about me or my business?

_____

_____

    Why am I doing this here and why now?

    _____

    _____

What is the attribute? Where and when will I present this quality attribute about me or my business?

_____

_____

    Why am I doing this here and why now?

    _____

    _____

As a suggestion to you, you might want to build what salespeople call an "Evidence Manual" for customers to look through. An "Evidence Manual" is a scrap book in which you put letters of recommendation from customers in as well as anything else that might build value in your product, service, your business, or yourself.

You could put in a photo from the little league team you sponsor, positive articles about you, your store, or your product. Anything that might add value.

Just as earlier, think about when you would like to have your customer look at this book. It can keep them busy if there is a delay of some kind in the process. Are they waiting for a car? A stereo installation? A business manager? A technician?

You could also post this information on the web and send them the link if you do business over the telephone or through your website.

Find a way to sell yourself and build value. You have done a great job throughout your process. It's time to close the deal.

The nice thing is, once you've put together the information and your process, you don't have to keep rebuilding it. You only need to tweak the process from time to time and update the information every so often. All depending on how the business changes.

It'll get easier. You're going to have to trust me on that.
Keep on going forward!

- Tip 64: Build value in yourself and your business.
- Tip 65: Know when to present this information.
- Tip 66: You are unique and have things to offer that others can't.

"People might buy from a place the first time because of price, a repeat sale will be because of the experience and the salesperson."

- *Rip Walker*

Chapter 15: What is Your Closing Process?

Closing happens throughout the sales process. The ads on TV, the style of your store, your company's web site, and the brochures that are offered to customers are all trying to close a sale.

You've heard the phrase, "Always be closing!" It's true, but that phrase seems to create an image of some slick, snake oil salesman swindling people into giving up hard earned cash for a worthless product. That's not what we're talking about here.

We're talking about making it conducive for people to buy. By having a good sales process that includes building value in your product or service, your company, and yourself, you are always closing.

Closing a sale refers to helping a customer decide on your product or service, you, and your company. They need to feel that your product or service is right for them, and they are getting what they want or need.

Keep in mind that sales, is a noble occupation and when the sales drop, the economy stops. Just look at anytime car and home sales drop. It can be pretty scary.

If you've been selling for a while, think of the times when it almost seemed too easy of a sale. Maybe you sold a house or a car or an expensive TV and you kind of just flowed through the deal. Your customer signed off on the buyer's order or contract without blinking an eye. What happened? Why was it easy?

Most likely you followed a well executed sales process. Most of the possible objections were handled during the process.

Your customers were put in a positive state of mind. They were saying yes to you and yes to your offering. What I'm saying here is that all the little agreements you got along the way, got you the big one later in the process.

The customer said, "Yes, I like this salesperson. He or she knows what they are doing." And, "Yes, it will work for me." Or, "Yes. This is the type of outfit I want to deal with."

Just think for a moment, what if they are saying no during the process? Do you think that you might have a tough time wrapping the sale up later? What do we do?

As I mentioned, we need the customer to be saying yes during the process. And it doesn't necessarily mean a yes to anything about you, or what you are selling. Much of it is psychological. All of us get a bit defensive when we walk into a store where we fear that we might be sold into something we don't want or need.

As part of your process, we need to get customers to say yes, and it can be about anything. "Good morning!" "Boy it's sunny outside!" And they respond yes, because it is sunny. "Look how it's raining outside!" And they say yes, because it is raining.

You see what I did. I just changed my question to get a positive affirmation. During your process, what type of questions can you ask to get a yes? We'll get into how to handle a "**No**" later, but for now what questions can you ask that most likely will get you a yes?

You already know why you are asking these questions. Write out a few now on the lines below. Keep in mind, try to ask questions in which you know the probable answer. It's been written that you should only ask questions in which you know the answer, but that only works in an ideal world. It's a nice theory.

Try not to ask questions that will get you a negative response and be careful if you decide to ask, "How are you today?" You never know what you're gonna get.

My "Yes" Questions: Write a few questions that you think that you will get a **"Yes"** response.

Example: "It's sunny isn't it?" "It looks like a great weekend?" "Does the seat feel good?" "Does it have the features you like?" "Does this suit your needs?"

1. _____
2. _____
3. _____
4. _____
5. _____

Where in your process are you going to use these questions? Use common sense and apply a **"Yes"** question where appropriate.

At First Impression

My **"Yes"** questions:

_____

_____

_____

At Discovery

My **"Yes"** questions:

_____

_____

_____

During My Presentation

My **"Yes"** questions:

_____

_____

_____

During My Recommendation

My **"Yes"** questions:

_____

_____

_____

When I Sell Myself and My Company

My **"Yes"** questions:

_____

_____

_____

Looks like your process is taking shape. Creating a process is a process itself. You've broken it down into smaller parts with goals in each section. You then have written the steps and why you do what you do. You're almost there.

The Negotiation Process

You've been doing your little closes throughout your process. You feel good and the customer seems to like you. Now it's time for the numbers. You print up or write up the buyer's agreement, the order or whatever you call it in your business. You now go to present it to your customer. How do you present your offer?

There are probably one thousand different ways. Use common sense and build an effective one for yourself or your business. Keep in mind that at this is the point where there will be some tension.

People are very touchy about politics, religion, and their money. Money is also important to everybody for different reasons. But for the most part, money directly affects their lifestyle.

Hopefully, you've reduced much of the tension already, and you don't want it rise too much during this part of the process. Back to basics, we need to answer the questions of where, what, when, and how?

Keeping the theories that we discussed earlier, let's put together your negotiation process. I've given you a few questions to get you thinking.

Step 1: Where am I going to negotiate?

_____

_____

Why am I doing it here? It's more conducive to the process? I don't have a choice?

_____

_____

Step 2: What will I say or do next? Will I present numbers? On paper?

_____

_____

Why am I doing this?

_____

_____

Step 3: What will I say or do next? Will I present the numbers? Will my manager?

_____

_____

Why am I doing this?

_____

_____

Step 4: What will I say or do next? How are the numbers presented?

_____

_____

Why am I doing this?

_____

_____

Step 5: What will I say or do next? What if they said yes? No?

_____

_____

Why am I doing this?

_____

_____

Wow! It takes a lot of thought to actually put a process to writing. As I said, you're almost there, don't quit now.

Handling a No

In Chapter 2: *Understand the Basics of a Process,* we briefly discussed handling objections. If you have followed a good sales process and have gotten yes answers, you might need only to ask for the order. We all wish it was that simple.

One thing that we should all understand is that you won't close them all. As good as the product or service is that you have, it just won't happen. If you truly don't offer what's needed, you probably won't close the deal.

When someone does actually buy the wrong product, the customer will eventually wake up to the fact and become dissatisfied with the product.

I recently needed to cut some dead trees down in my backyard, so I decided to purchase a chainsaw. I went to *Lowe's* to look for one and went with a cheaper, electric chainsaw. It couldn't handle the work, and it burned out within a few uses. How do you think I felt?

Lowe's has outstanding customer service. Returning the remains of the electric chainsaw wasn't a problem. The manager came over and gave me cash.

We talked about chainsaws for a few moments, he asked me questions about what I would use the saw for, and he recommended a gas powered model.

He said that it was about $200 more, but it would last forever and cut down just about anything I had in my backyard. It was some of the best money I had spent. Timber!

As far as the original electric chainsaw that I bought, I will not buy anything made by that company again. I was totally dissatisfied with the product.

Just a note on shopping at a self serve operations, get help from their people when you are going to buy something that you are unfamiliar with. If I had taken a few minutes with a person in the right department, I wouldn't have wasted my time and been dissatisfied by what I bought.

As for *Lowe's*, I am a loyal fan of their stores. Most of my experiences with them have been outstanding. I've spent thousands and thousands of dollars there, and they offer a great customer experience. Great job!

All of that to say this, you can't win them all. It may be the product or service. Maybe it's your hair style or lack of hair. It doesn't matter. What matters is having a sales process which will increase the odds of closing the sale.

A "No" can happen anywhere in the sales process. Some you can handle at that moment, some will have to wait until a different point in the process, and some aren't a real "No" to begin with.

A "No" is an objection. Here are the simple steps to handle an objection:

1. Acknowledge the objection.
2. Find out the "Why."
3. Confirm what the objection is.
4. Offer an answer or do something to solve the objection.
5. Get a yes to verify that the objection was answered.

Here's an example, with analysis:

Salesperson: Does the seat feel comfortable?

The salesperson asks a question to get a yes.

Customer: No, it doesn't feel right.

The customer says, "No." This objection came up after trying to get a "Yes."

Salesperson: You don't think that it feels right?

Here, the salesperson **acknowledges the objection** by repeating what the customer said.

Customer: Yep.

The customer answers yes, because the salesperson phrased his question to get one.

Salesperson: What doesn't feel right about it?

The salesperson looks to **find the "Why."** Without knowing the "Why," he can't answer the objection.

Customer: The seat is too low.

The salesperson now has the "Why" and can proceed.

Salesperson: The seat is too low?

The salesperson **confirms the objection** with the customer.

Customer: Yeah.

And another yes!

Salesperson: The seat has an adjustment to raise the seat. Let's try this. (The salesperson adjusts the seat.) How is it now?

The salesperson **solves the specific objection** by adjusting the seat. And, if he didn't know that the seat had a height adjustment, the sale might be lost. Remember to know about what you are selling.

Customer: That's better.

Salesperson: So the seat feels good now.

The salesperson **verifies that the objection was answered** and he goes for a "Yes."

Customer: Yes.

And another close it is.

When you try to handle an objection, the customer may not be satisfied with your solution. You will then need to repeat this process and get more information. Don't be afraid to repeat the process, because you'll need to repeat it throughout your sales process to get **"Yes"** answers.

As a salesperson you need to be persistent. Good salespeople will ask at least six times for the sale. Don't be shy and don't let anybody else take your earned commission.

What's your closing process? With all of the different things that you can do to answer an objection, there is no cookie cutter way to handle all of them. Just remember that the basics are the same.

Even with a price objection, the process is the same. Acknowledge the objection and find out the **"Why."** Different information will require different answers.

If the customer is comparing apples to oranges, you may need to explain some differences between the products and why your product is worth more money.

If the products are identical, you might build more value in yourself or in your company.

If it's too much money, you may go to your switch product or offer a different one.

In the end, maybe you will have to close the deal on a price, but a good salesperson will try to hold his gross profit before going to a discount. Don't be lazy! Take your best shot and follow your process.

Fill in the blanks below with a response to your number one objection.

What is the objection that I get the most from my customers?

_____

_____

What will I say to acknowledge the objection? What statement will I use?

_____

_____

What question will I use to find the specific objection? What is the "Why?"

_____

_____

What will I say to confirm the objection?

_____

_____

What will my solution or answer be for that objection?

_____

_____

What will I ask to verify that the objection was answered? What will I say to get a "Yes?"

_____

_____

What will I do if they still say "No?"

_____

_____

Looks like you have an objection handling process.

Remember that in addition to having a good process, you must be knowledgeable about your product, service, your business, and the competition to be more successful.

You may have noticed that handing an objection is similar in structure to a needs assessment and a recommendation. They are very much alike, because they are about communication skills. Once you have one of these processes down, the others will become easier as well.

You're doing a great job! As I said, once you have your process in writing, life will become better. Selling isn't so tough once you have your plan.

- Tip 67: Be knowledgeable about what you sell.
- Tip 68: Be persistent and ask for the sale repeatedly.
- Tip 69: Different objections have different answers.

*"People will narrow their buying choices with logic,
but will purchase based on how they feel."*

- *Rip Walker*

Chapter 16: How Will You Deliver Your Product or Service?

They said yes and signed the deal. What do you do now? You might want to review what you thought was important and needed to give your customer a great last impression. As with any part of this, what are your goals for this part of the process?

Goals

Some possible goals to achieve at delivery and to achieve a great last impression could be to…

1. Have the customer enjoy themselves.
2. Have them remember you.
3. Have them become familiar with their purchase.
4. Have them get familiar with support.
5. Have them purchase add-ons.

What do you want to achieve?

1. _____
2. _____
3. _____
4. _____
5. _____

You should be pretty good at writing out your process at this point in the book. The format is the same as any process. Just write answers to the questions about what to do and why. I've included a few thought starters by each step.

My Delivery Process

Step 1: Where will you deliver? At the customer's location, your store, or in a warehouse? Will they receive the goods at their house? Will your service people be conducting the service at another location?

_____

_____

Why am I delivering there? Is it more conducive? It's where the product is? Is it where the service will take place?

_____

_____

Step 2:What will I say or do next? What will I cover?

_____

_____

Why am I doing this?

_____

_____

Step 3: What will I say or do next? What will I show them?

143

_____

_____

     Why am I doing this?

     _____

     _____

Step 4: What will I say or do next? Will I share any company service information?

_____

_____

     Why am I doing this?

     _____

     _____

Step 5: What will I say or do next? Any forms to fill out?

_____

_____

     Why am I doing this?

     _____

     _____

Step 6: What will I say or do next? Do I put the customer in a database?

_____

_____

     Why am I doing this?

     _____

     _____

Step 7: What will I say or do next? Do I do any introductions?

_____

_____

    Why am I doing this?

    _____

    _____

Step 8: What will I say or do next? Do I set up any follow up?

_____

_____

    Why am I doing this?

    _____

    _____

Step 9: What will I say or do next? Does the customer need anything?

_____

_____

    Why am I doing this?

    _____

    _____

Step 10: What will I say or do next? What else? What else? What else?

_____

_____

Why am I doing this?

_____

_____

You now have delivered your product, made the sale, or the service has been completed. By the way, if you sold a service that you will be doing yourself, I would highly recommend that you write out the directions in depth just as you have with your sales process. If someone else ever does the service for you, they'll need good directions.

A process can't be repeated in a consistent manner if you don't put it in writing. When you teach someone about your process, remember to tell them **"Why"** they are doing each step.

The deal is done right? Are you moving onto the next customer, the next sale, the next commission?

A good, professional salesperson will tell you that you've just begun. To really make a decent buck you have to have repeat customers and referrals. And you can create a process for that.

Your customer has had that great 1st class service from you and your outfit, and they are enjoying the fruits of their labors with the new product or service.

To get the additional business you need them to remember not just your company, but more important you!

How do you do that? How do you get the customer to remember you? Next chapter please!

- Tip 70: Remember to give your customers a great last impression.
- Tip 71: A process can't be repeated in a consistent manner if you don't put it in writing.
- Tip 72: Your customers need to remember you.

"Remember, people will judge you by your actions, not your intentions. You may have a heart of gold -- but so does a hard-boiled egg."

- *Anonymous*

Chapter 17: How Will Your Customer Remember You?

If you want to make more money, if you're tired of living off of what is coming through the door, or if you just want your life to be easier with fewer hassles, this chapter is for you.

To be really successful in sales, your customers need to remember you. We can create a process for doing that. It's just another process, but let's go through a few ways before you decide how you are going to build this process. First, a story.

Do I really need a story here to emphasize the importance of calling people back and following up? That it makes common sense to do these things? I'm going to give you one anyway.

I was a moving salesperson at the time. We'll say that the customer's name was Mr. Smith. I had sold Mr. Smith a move a year earlier, and it didn't go very well. If something could have gone wrong with his relocation, it did.

I blew the estimate and cost. The driver broke his furniture and damaged Mr. Smith's new home. I had apologized and the company really tried to make him happy, but Mr. Smith complained for what must have been months. I held his hand through the entire debacle. I was very happy when his calls to complain subsided.

One day, I received a message from him to call. I just said, "Crap, when will this be over?" I stalled calling him back for three days. I finally called and he didn't call to complain.

He called because his mother was retiring to Florida. He was handing me a sale, but because I was such a chicken, I almost lost it. Calling back will make you money, its common sense.

Calling people back is a professional act and appreciated by many. It's all part of follow up.

I'm not saying just call to say hi just and shoot the breeze. It needs to be a value call. Always have something of value to give your customers. It might just be to offer some new information or answer some questions.

Again, **"You"** have to do it.

Following Up

This goes hand in hand with calling people back, but there is more to it. Follow up doesn't mean just staying in touch with active customers. It also means staying in touch with past customers and prospective customers as well. We've already discussed calling customers back. Let's look at an example in regard to following up.

I was speaking with a real estate salesperson a while back. The man had been in the business for over twenty years and has seen it boom and bust. I was wondering how he kept an even keel through tough times.

He told me about his follow up program. He said how unfortunate it is that so many of us learn by mistakes. Sometimes we learn the hard way, but we learn just the same.

When he started, he courted this couple around for months. The young couple finally found a place that they could call home. Unfortunately, they bought a house directly from an owner. No commission, just a very nice thank you note from them for the help. He threw the note in a trash basket.

To grind additional salt in his wounds, they would call once in a while and ask him if he could give a recommendation for an electrician. Then it was a plumber. Then it was a car salesperson. Fortunately it was me.

My friend was a nice guy, so he always helped them out. Then one day, a few years later, they called him again. They asked him about a house in a very exclusive part of town. My friend said that he would check into it.

This is the part of the story where I'm supposed to tell you how he lost the sale because he just wouldn't follow up.

Actually, that's not the case. He went out with them and sold them the house and got his commission.

Sometimes, by pure luck we sell something. In this case, the customers were following up with him. That's not how it usually works.

After that experience, my friend started a follow up system. He would send out a newsletter, not just to sold customers, but to ones who didn't buy from him as well. Point is, follow up with everybody, even if they don't buy from you.

Most customers will buy again if you hang around long enough. Having great follow up is common sense.

Remember that the main reason for following up is so that the customer will remember you for their next purchase or for referrals. They'll remember the store or the business, but you have to have a process so you get the next sale.

Let's look at some of the best ways that we can follow up. First, look at your business to decide what are the best methods for you to stay in touch. If you're selling cars and do a bang up job, email will be the number one ticket.

If you are selling multi-million dollar computer systems or something else where there are far fewer customers, you will need a much more personnel approach and that would include more time on the phone and some first class mail.

On an individual basis let's look at each one.

Mail

In most cases, mail had its day before email. I'm not saying don't send a birthday or anniversary card to our customers, they're great.

Send a birthday card to a customer who you sold something to and their spouse forgets the date, and you will own that customer for life. Well, at least until death do us part or a divorce.

However, we want to utilize more common sense.

Mail has just gotten so expensive. Your boss may not be too happy to pay for it. Again, depending on what you are selling you will have to decide. If I'm selling *Lear* jets, I would spring for the first class postage.

Email

When we talked about building a client base, we suggested staying in touch by email. Everybody gets email, it's cheap, and it can be very effective.

Even so, don't become SPAM! If a person does a click or two and labels you SPAM, your emails will be wasted. We all get way too many emails. With a communication to your customer, you have to give them value, and you don't need to be a pain. That's common sense.

Take my real estate agent friend, create a newsletter to stay in touch with your customers. Email once a month. Always, try to send them information that they can use. Be creative, if it's ways for them to save money great! If it's ways to make life easier better! Offer benefits!

As long as they don't put you in the SPAM can, it's done its job. Remember, that you just want to keep your name in front of them. They need to remember you!

Websites

I would also recommend that you get computer savvy and build a web site, if your company doesn't have one already. To really be successful you will need to be creative or find somebody who is creative to help you. You can get a *Yahoo* website on the cheap to start you off.

And it needs to have the same principle as the newsletter. There has to be a benefit for people to go to your site. Think of what you can give, or what you can offer.

Of course, put your pretty face there with contact information and information that would be helpful to your customers. What about service and support or **"How to do,"** web videos? You don't have to film them, just post the links, so they can find them.

Use corporate sites as an example. As an individual, I just want to keep it simple with low maintenance. Post a few links every other week, maybe a list of inventory or new services, and a newsletter. Nothing crazy! A good size company can do a lot more.

I was helping to create a training website for the company I worked for. It was a lot of work. I couldn't keep up with the videos that needed to be produced. However, the main manufacturer for our product started to produce all the videos that I needed. I just posted the links to them, and it made my life a whole lot simpler.

Telephone

Just a short note here. Use telephone etiquette and offer value on the phone as well as in emails and your website.

When you make a call, there are some rules that you should follow. Please, take a look at mine.

Rip's Telephone Rules

1. **Ask for the person that you need to speak with.** If you end up speaking with the wrong person, you've wasted everyone's time. For example, a few years ago I got a bill from the cable company. I was getting billed for some adult channels that I didn't order.

   It turned out when they had called, they got my son, who has the same name as me. (His voice at sixteen was deeper than mine.)

   They asked if he would like any special "Packages." Well, a sixteen year old boy offered adult programming? You know the rest of the story. It took me over six months to get those channels canceled and blocked.

2. **Ask for permission to speak with them.** In most cases, you will be interrupting something. Dinner? Lunch? A meeting? Do you really want to speak with someone that won't be listening to you anyway? I didn't think so.

   Ask them, "Am I interrupting anything important?" Again, you are interrupting something, but let the customer decide. If they give you permission, get to the point. Do they have any questions? Ask for the sale? Etc.

3. **Thank them for their time.** People appreciate professionalism and politeness. Don't' forget what your mother told you.

Follow up is common sense and to do it efficiently and in a professional manner is even better!

- Tip 73: Call people back.
- Tip 74: Get or create a follow up system.
- Tip 75: Offer value in your correspondence.
- Tip 76: Follow telephone rules.

"Price is soon forgotten, but the experience and value of the purchase will long be remembered."

- Rip Walker

Chapter 18: How Do I Build My Customer Base?

Some time ago I was selling cars and the district factory representative came into see our sales team and speak with us about customer satisfaction. As salespeople we were really curious about what the factory had to say to us.

Ten of us, plus the factory representative, crammed into the Business Manager's wood paneled office. We had a conference table put in the room for this big meeting.

The representative introduced himself, paused, and then threw a customer satisfaction report on the table.

He said, "What the hell are you guys doing to people?" There wasn't even a pause. We all started laughing hard. The poor factory representative just shook his head and left.

You see, things like customer satisfaction have to come from the top down. Our customer satisfaction ratings were some of the lowest in the country. It was a joke.

The owner at the time was making buckets of money. Plenty of buyers at the time and he would never be in store to take the heat. Our motto was, "Hold them until they scream." I guess that wasn't very customer friendly.

Needless to say, we didn't do much in the way of repeat business. None of us would build a customer base, because who would want to get taken a second time? I apologize to anyone that bought a car from me there.

Let's fast forward to another dealership. I had been there for years, did my follow up, built a customer base, and I carried one of the highest customer satisfaction ratings in the country for *Toyota* at that time.

One day when I was down a bit, for whatever reason, in walks a customer. He asks the receptionist for me, and she directs him over. Understand, I was really feeling down. But, the customer was excited.

He says, "Are you Rip Walker?" I say, "Yeah."

He said, "There's a red truck out there I want to buy."

I ask, "Did you get the stock number?"

He says, "Yep." And he hands me the number scribbled on a piece of paper.

I didn't even get off my butt to offer him a test drive. This is not the way to treat someone, but the point of this story is not about my crummy attitude that day. I did need an attitude adjustment that day, but that's not the moral to the story.

I proceeded to write up the deal and deliver the truck. It was a very easy deal, no brain damage.

Here's the moral. Build a good customer base and you don't have to work as hard. You can even be off a bit and still write business. You can make more money and have more fun. You should still treat your customers like gold, but I think that you get the idea.

Let's use our common sense and talk about ways to build a client base.

Build One From Scratch

To build one takes a lot of time, effort, and work. It's real simple. As you sell, you build the relationship with each customer.

It works! I've done it and you should be doing it anyway. However, you will probably grow old and not live life to the fullest.

As earlier, salespeople should stay in touch with unsold customers as well. There's a good chance that the salesperson they bought from won't do the follow up, or they will tick that customer off at some point. You need to be in the wings for the next opportunity.

Here are some of the better ways to build a customer base!

Buy One

Buy a "Book of Business." For those of you who have worked in the insurance industry, you may already know about this.

Simply contact someone who already has a large customer base and is willing to sell it to you. Be aware that it can get very expensive, but it can be effective if done properly.

I once knew an insurance agent who grew her insurance agency by doing that. She made so much money that she has continued to expand and grow. She has done very well for herself, and I admire anyone that works hard and strives to achieve.

You can do the same thing, but, be careful! Get the information to make a good choice. How many people in their base? How long have they been in the business? Will the person be selling the business to you sign a non-compete agreement? (If they won't agree to that one, don't bother. You don't want them reopening next door to you.) Is everything on the up and up?

Again, be very careful! You really need to know the people that you are dealing with.

Get One

And I mean to get one for free! Yes, it might take a little work, but you can do this in just about any business.

With all the computers and databases life is simpler. Here's what you can do to build your base quickly.

Most retail businesses have a database already in place and should have been taking customers' information for years.

Remember that these are customers, which already have a relationship with the company that you are working for. You just need to step in and pick up the ball.

Here are some steps that you can take:

1. **You** have whoever manages the customer database, replace the old salesperson's name with your name in the database.
2. **You** write a nice introductory letter to introduce you as the customer's new salesperson.
3. **You** have it mail merged with the database.
4. **You** send the letter out.
5. **You** call to introduce yourself and ask if there is anything that you can do for them.
6. **You** follow up and take care of whatever the issue was.
7. **You** call to thank them again and to see if there is anything else that you can do.
8. **You** stay in touch through mail or email.
9. Oh yeah! **You** may have a sale!

Since I am a big proponent of knowing what you are doing and why, please let me explain a bit further.

One day, when I was whining about the unfairness of life to my dad, he looked at me and said, "Right now you are sitting on the only real security that you have in life."

I asked him, "What does that mean?"

He turned to me, reached behind his back and grabbed a good part of his right butt cheek and continued, "You have to take responsibility, grab life and do it! This is your security!"

It took me a second to figure this one out, but it meant that I was the only thing that was really secure. Things happen to people, but you have to take responsibility for your life and what happens. You have to make things happen.

I highlighted **"You,"** because **"You"** are the one that's going to make things happen. For anything that you might want to get done, please feel free to reach around your back and get your butt in motion. We all need to be reminded of this on occasion, including myself.

What is your plan to build your customer base? Circle one or write one out.

1. I'll Build One.
2. I'll Buy One.
3. I'll get One For Free.
4. I'll do something else.

_____

_____

Here's something you need to learn from someone else's mistake. It's related to building your customer base. It's common sense not to cold call!

Not to Cold Call

Hopefully, this is almost a thing of the past, but who knows?

There was a time when, as a salesperson, you would be handed the phone book and told to call all the A's, then the B's, etc.

When I started in the car business so long ago, it was actually a somewhat effective way to prospect for new business. A cold call is when you arbitrarily call or contact someone to solicit their business out of nowhere.

The problem was, with more and more competition it became less effective. Cold calls are not effective and a waste of time, except for maybe the owner, who pays only on commission and has an entire team of underpaid phone solicitors.

It pays to make **"Hot Calls and Contacts."** Many sales gurus say warm calls. With the information that is available to everyone, you need to make **"Hot Calls and Contacts."** These are calls or contacts that really have a chance of being successful. Remember, common sense.

You need to get as much information that you can about your prospect. I started at one dealership and the first thing that I asked for was all of their **"Owner Orphans." "Orphan Owners"** are people, who bought something from the business, but their salesperson is no longer there.

The sales manager at a store that had started working at, laughed when I asked for them. I asked why? He told me that none of the salespeople followed up on them, and that I could have them all.

Now this was when personal computers were just starting to come out, so there was no database where I could just punch a few buttons and gather the information. I had to crawl into the attic, pull files, and make copies of each deal.

I then plugged them into my hand-me-down computer at home and created a mailing list for my monthly newsletter. I sent over 2000 letters out that month.

I ended up with a *Toyota Landcruiser* deal. I made my mortgage and the owner didn't mind the $600 postage bill at all.

One of the best parts was watching another salesperson complain to the sales manager about how he should get part of the deal, because he helped deliver the customer's last car several years ago.

The sales manager asked him when was the last time that he had contacted this customer. Sorry, but he didn't do his follow up, but that's not the point of this story. The point is that I made **"Hot Calls and Contacts."** They are definitely more successful. Use common sense and don't waste your time.

The other information that I had, once I reviewed the files, was the financial information of these customers. I had a good idea about what they could finance.

In one case, after reviewing ten years of a customer's file, I found that the person's credit was getting better and better. Originally, the customer had some bad marks on his credit, but by the time I would sell him a car he could pretty much buy what he wanted. Cool!

There are more benefits for you in that customer database. Just look and cross reference. Where do they work? Where do they live? Make your life easier and analysis your information at hand.

Now that you've built a database and can analysis the information, you can make **"Hot Calls and Contacts."**

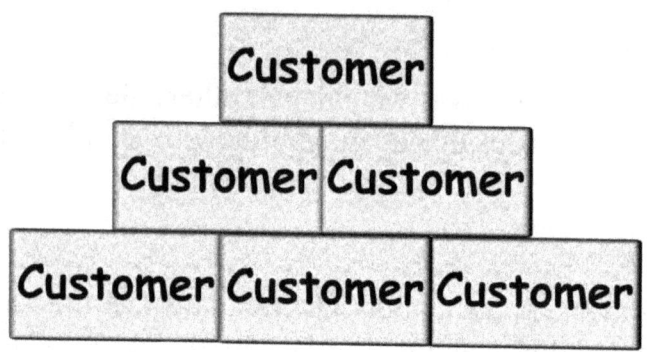

- Tip 77: Having a customer base makes life easier.
- Tip 78: Get a customer base.
- Tip 79: Have a plan to stay in touch with your customers.
- Tip 80: Make *"Hot Calls and Contacts."*
- Tip 81: Analysis your database.
- Tip 82: Working efficiently pays off.

"Right now you are sitting on the only real security that you have in life."

- *William J. Walker*

Section III: For Your Future and Continuing Success

Continue learning, be yourself, be sincere, and realize that there are things greater than us all. The words sound motivational and they are meant to be. In the next few pages we'll spend some time with these words.

What I would ask now is that you take a look at where you are in your life. It doesn't matter what age, whether you're married, or whether you have kids or not. Just think for a second and think about where you are right now.

Ask yourself this: Are you happy with what you have and where you are? It's okay if you are, but most people want more. Maybe it's a better car? Maybe it's a better house? Maybe it's a better lifestyle? Maybe it's more time to do what you would rather be doing? Whatever it is, it's okay. The point that I am getting to is what motivates you? What will drive you?

We discussed goals in regard to process, but what about your own personal goals? All that I ask you to do is write them down. It's the same as developing and creating a process for sales. You're just creating the directions to where you want to go in life.

When you set a goal it needs to be specific. Don't just say, "I want more money." What's the number? $10,000 more a year? $50,000 more? "I want a better job." Do you want to be a manager? A doctor? Do you want a house? Where?

Be specific when you list out your goals, because you're going to be specific in your directions. The more carefully thought out your "Lifestyle Improvement" process, the more likely you will hit your goal. Remember what my dad said, "Wishing for it ain't gonna make it happen."

Goals

Some possible goals for people could be:

1. I want to make $10,000 more per year.
2. I want to take my family to Disney World.
3. I want a new computer.
4. I want to get a college degree.

What do you want to achieve?

1. _____
2. _____
3. _____
4. _____
5. _____

The format to achieve your goals is the same as any process. Write out what you want, and what you need to do to get there. It could take some research to find out how to reach your goal as well.

Make a commitment and put your process in writing. You never know what you can achieve. Write it out, take responsibility, and take action. Go!

My "Lifestyle Improvement" Process

What is your specific goal?

_____

_____

      Why do I want this? Will I be happier? Will my life
      be easier? Will my family be more secure?

      _____

      _____

Step 1: What do I need to do first to get it done?

_____

_____

      Why am I doing this?

      _____

      _____

Step 2: What do I need to do next?

_____

_____

      Why am I doing this?

      _____

      _____

Step 3: What do I need to do next?

_____

_____

Why am I doing this?

_____

_____

Step 4: What do I need to do next?

_____

_____

Why am I doing this?

_____

_____

Step 5: What do I need to do next?

_____

_____

Why am I doing this?

_____

_____

If there are not enough blanks here, write them out on a note pad and continue.

Final Step: How will I know when I achieve my goal? Will the money be in my account? Will I have it in my hands? Will I have a degree? Will I have a new title? A new job? Be specific.

_____

_____

You now have goals for your future and a plan. Don't get too upset if somewhere down the road something happens, and you need to change your goals or plans. Life happens.

I was married for about 23 years, which essentially sent me in a different direction than I originally planned, but it was just a long delay. I'm back in the right direction, and it wasn't all bad. I have three great kids to show for my efforts.

The final chapters are designed to help you move forward and help you achieve your goals. Grab your butt and get going!

- Tip 83: Set specific goals.
- Tip 84: Write down your goals and how you'll achieve them.
- Tip 85: Describe how you will know when you hit your goal.

"Specific goals give direction, motivation, and purpose."

- *Rip Walker*

Chapter 19: Continue to Learn

*"Professionals know what they do and
why they do it that way."*

Some people get away with just talent and some with shear heart. And some people are successful with a combination of them. But, to be the best or to do your very best, you have to know not just what you are doing, but also why you do it the way you do.

Do you think that *Tiger Woods* just swings away? Do you think that *Jeff Gordon* just points a car around the track and pushes the gas pedal to the floor? Do you think that *Michael Jordan* just relied on his talent?

All are talented, but all are students of the game. These people study and work on their craft. Yes, they are all extremely talented. But, they all continue to learn and develop themselves.

Enough said, but let see just how we can learn these days.

On the Job

If you are working, there may be opportunities right where you are. Most of my training was right at work. There were online programs, mentor programs, and classroom education. Some training was in-house and some from the outside.

The company even paid for me to take two years of Spanish, which was really helpful when I did business in South Florida. Thank you.

Academic Institutions

Everybody knows about the local college or adult training that's around where you live. If you don't, take a look on the web, and you'll find a multitude of offerings.

What many people use as an excuse is they think that it will cost too much. When my son was a senior in high school, we attended a recruitment meeting for *University of Miami*. I took the speaker's words to heart. He said, "Do not, not apply because of the money."

My son had great grades and had worked his butt off in high school. The estimated $40,000 dollars per year college cost at Miami was daunting, but apply, we did.

Florida has a great program for good students, it's called *Bright Futures*. Do well in school and you get money for college.

Okay, that was bout 5K yearly. With his awesome grade point average, my son would receive about 20K yearly from the university. 15K to go. He attends a UM Business School open house, seems there's another 5K a year available if you write a great essay.

After all was said and done, there was relatively not much left; Okay, he has a school loan, but he was offered a great job at *Goldman Sachs* after graduation. I think that he'll be able to pay it off. Point is, don't give up because of the money!

There's money available and you don't have to attend an Ivy League school. My wife is attending school for low cost at the community college. She also received some funding. I will tell you right now, you will have to dig. Don't give up!

From Mentors

There are mentoring programs and business groups that can help you. Try the local Chamber of Commerce. Try learning from an expert at work. Just ask and you might receive.

When you attend a sales meeting, ask the best what they do. How do they sell? What makes them successful? Many will be glad to help. Ignore the ones that won't. Remember, that you are responsible for yourself.

Self Taught

There is so much available out there for our self improvement. The web offers tons of material on whatever you do.

There are periodicals and publications available to you from just about every industry. Many end up, for some reason, in the customer lounge areas. The problem is that many people don't take advantage of the information. Motivate yourself to read articles from these publications.

Or, how about reading a book for self improvement? It's a novel idea isn't it? Pardon the pun. I do suggest that you read frequently for self improvement, but I'll also suggest that you try to find a style of books that you like.

For example, I've used stories to help make the points in this book. If you don't like this style, there might be something more text book. That's okay, find a style or find an author that you like. One that you enjoy.

We learn by picking up ideas that relate to us. Don't expect to remember everything from what you read, or what you hear in a class. With experience, you'll find that you'll pick up an idea here and an idea there. That's the reality.

Try to look at it this way, if you go to a training, read a book or a related publication, and pick up one useful idea, it will be well worth your efforts, and it will reflect in your future endeavors.

Hopefully, some of the tips I've given you will help you out.

- Tip 86: Money is available for education. Dig!
- Tip 87: Read related publications, books, and articles to aid in your development.
- Tip 88: If you pick up one idea from a training, a book or a publication, it was well worth your efforts.

*"Continue to learn and
you continue to grow."*

- Rip Walker

Chapter 20: Be Yourself and Be Sincere

Many people live double lives. I'm not talking about serial killers, I'm talking about every day people. Some people have to be different at home than at any other place. Many are closest to being themselves at work.

It can be very difficult when the two meet on occasion at a company Christmas party. Spouses don't understand why people are so friendly with you. This brings conflict and creates a knot in the pit of your stomach. It's hard to be two people. Some of this information should be spared for some type of self help marital book, but to let's get to the point.

Try to be yourself and be sincere with everybody. It's pretty self explanatory. Aside from what it does to us, most people can tell when you're not really being sincere or being yourself. I'm not sure how they figure it out.

It's probably a few things like non-verbal cues, body language, tone of voice, and lack of eye contact. Of course, that's just me talking. When people see this in a salesperson they can decide to go elsewhere.

I'm sure that we've all heard this before, but I'm going to tell you again anyway. You have to be true to yourself and be what you are. You will never be truly happy and pursue what you want in life if you don't. It took me a long time to accept myself. I don't want others to go through the same thing.

I now take the responsibility for where I am in life, and what I'm doing. I have goals that I wish to achieve. I want to be a writer of books and screenplays. I want to make a living doing my passion.

If you're reading this, it tells you that the book has been published, someone has paid for it, and it has put me on my way to becoming a working, self supporting writer. How about that? One goal down.

My goals include being a writer, but they also include helping my wife get her law degree, teaching all of our kids how to be self sufficient, to live comfortably, and do some travel.

Yes, I do need some money to do that, and my wife and I have some plans in place to achieve not just my goals, but my wife's goals as well.

And it's not all me. My wife is 125% supportive of my efforts. She hasn't thrown me one negative in the time that I've known her. She's amazing.

Quite frankly, if you don't have the full support of your family for what you want to achieve, you'll compromise in too many areas, and most likely not achieve your goals. It's a fact of life.

By the way, there are plenty of negative people out there who say that everything is bad and that our society is doomed. If you accept what they say, you'll probably be with them in the lower levels of lifestyle. Please, take this advice and stay away from them. Try to keep positive people around you. It will work wonders for efforts towards success.

You can achieve your goals, but it will take planning and hard work. However, you need to be yourself and be sincere about who you are.

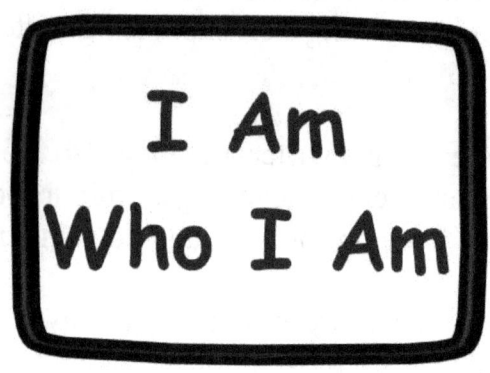

- Tip 89: Be yourself.
- Tip 90: Be sincere.
- Tip 91: Understand the facts of life.

"Sincerity makes the very least person to be of more value than the most talented hypocrite."

- *Charles Spurgeon*

Chapter 21: There are Things Greater Than All of Us

You've read the book this far, so don't stop now! Hopefully, you've picked up a few things. At this point, I want people to realize that there is more to life than just selling or any one particular thing, for that matter.

We are here for not even a moment in the timeline of infinity. What we do with our time is mostly up to us. Everyone has had a bit of bad luck somewhere along the way. Death of a loved one, divorce, sickness, job loss, etc… The list goes on.

We all get our bumps and bruises, but keep your chin up. Good things will happen to good people. It may take some time, but they will. And thank you for purchasing this book.

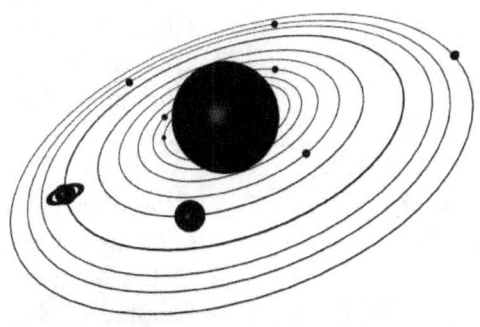

"We must take advantage of the opportunity that life has given us, because we won't get another one."

- Rip Walker

Index

Other Awesome Experiences

Innovation is taking an idea and applying it to something else. I didn't come up with all the ideas in this book. You should be doing the same with your processes, whether it be sales or some other type of process.

A great way to do this is by taking notes on the great experiences which you've had. Just write down what happened and the ideas that you might be able to use in your processes. Here's an example below.

Company: *Enterprise Rent a Car*

Date: July 6th, 2005

What happened?

I took my wife and my two daughters to NY, and we flew into Newark airport. I had booked a car with *Enterprise Rent-a-Car*, because of a slightly lower price.

I found that the *Enterprise* location in Newark was located close to the *Budweiser* plant in an area of Newark where I wouldn't want to find myself at night. In any case, we landed and took a shuttle tram to the offsite rent-a-car stop.

We got off the tram and then boarded a small shuttle bus to get taken over to the *Enterprise* location. We were tired and weren't looking forward to the usual hassle of waiting for a rental car.

Then something amazing happened when we arrived at their facility. There were three men wearing white shirts and ties standing by the shuttle door as we arrived.

As we left the shuttle, we greeted by these men. "Welcome to *Enterprise*, and your name is?" I responded, "Rip Walker." Do you have a reservation?" Again, I responded yes.

The next five minutes were a blur. He took our bags inside, took my license and credit card. Before I had a chance to sit down, he returned with paperwork, directed us out to the side of the building where the car would be, and then brought out our luggage.

The luggage was placed in the car along with my family. He took out a condition form and walked me around the car. We were looking to identify any damage that was already on the car.

I signed my paperwork, he shook my hand when I sat in the car, gave me exit and return directions, smiled, and thanked me for choosing *Enterprise*. Upon leaving, my wife asked me, in a good way, "What was that?" We were impressed to say the least.

In less than 5 minutes we were in and out. Wow! In contrast to the next week when I rented from another well known agency, and said that this 30 minute wait sucks, I should have rented from *Enterprise* again. I will forever more.

What ideas can I take from this experience? What can I be innovative with? What can I change and use in my business or process?

I've read about *Enterprise* and they are a leader in customer service. It was great to see that they practice what they preach in the books.

What I took back was how a well defined and executed process will do for the experience. I didn't realize just how bad the area was because of the experience.

They also set me up for a great experience later because of the directions that they gave me for my return to their location. Navigating around *Newark International Airport* can be confusing.

Their process was outstanding and the *Enterprise* employees executed the process flawlessly. They gave me a great experience all the way around. Great job!

This is the type of experience we need to take notes on. When you write them down, you don't need to be long winded, just make notes on what you thought were the best ideas.

Good luck in your search for awesome experiences!

Rip Walker

Your Awesome Experiences

Company: _____

Date: _____

What happened?

_____

_____

_____

_____

_____

_____

_____

_____

_____

_____

_____

What can I take from it and innovate it into my process?

_____

_____

_____

_____

_____

_____

_____

_____

_____

_____

_____

_____

Your Awesome Experiences

Company: _____

Date: _____

What happened?

_____

_____

_____

_____

_____

_____

_____

_____

_____

_____

What can I take from it and innovate it into my process?

_____

_____

_____

_____

_____

_____

_____

_____

_____

_____

_____

Your Awesome Experiences

Company: _____

Date: _____

What happened?

_____

_____

_____

_____

_____

_____

_____

_____

_____

_____

What can I take from it and innovate it into my process?

_____

_____

_____

_____

_____

_____

_____

_____

_____

_____

<u>Your Awesome Experiences</u>

Company: _____

Date: _____

What happened?

_____
_____
_____
_____
_____
_____
_____
_____
_____
_____

What can I take from it and innovate it into my process?

_____
_____
_____
_____
_____
_____
_____
_____
_____
_____
_____

Your Awesome Experiences

Company: _____

Date: _____

What happened?:

_____
_____
_____
_____
_____
_____
_____
_____
_____
_____

What can I take from it and innovate it into my process?

_____
_____
_____
_____
_____
_____
_____
_____
_____
_____
_____

www.ingramcontent.com/pod-product-compliance
Lightning Source LLC
Chambersburg PA
CBHW071425170526
45165CB00001B/400